Fearless Footsteps

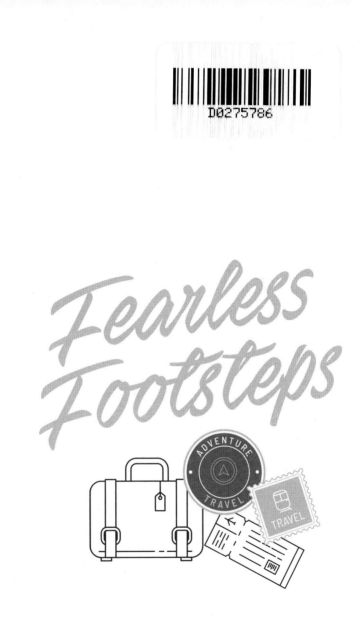

First published 2020

Exisle Publishing Pty Ltd
PO Box 864, Chatswood, NSW 2057, Australia
226 High Street, Dunedin, 9016, New Zealand
www.exislepublishing.com

A CiP record for this book is available from the National Library of
Australia.

ISBN 978-1-925820-57-7

Designed by www.bookdesigners.co
Typeset in Montserrat
Printed in China

This book uses paper sourced under ISO 14001 guidelines from
well-managed forests and other controlled sources.

10 9 8 7 6 5 4 3 2 1

Fearless Footsteps

true stories that capture the spirit of adventure

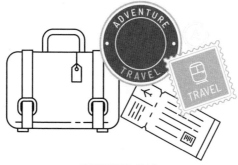

EDITED BY

NATHAN JAMES THOMAS & JENNIFER ROBERTS

EXISLE
PUBLISHING

Contents

Introduction

The difference between travel and adventure is the presence of fear. Here are the true stories of authors and wanderers who have encountered fear's diverse forms, from panic and paranoia to self-doubt and anxiety, yet continued their journey anyway. From the deserts of Namibia to the snowy plains of Antarctica, these stories cover every continent and have been carefully written and compiled to offer readers the chance to journey through fear and discover, on the other side, their own kind of adventure.

The stories in this anthology were collected as part of an international writing competition held by the online travel magazine, *Intrepid Times*. Writers were asked to share their stories about overcoming fear in whatever form that moved them. Inspiring tales of adventure landed in our inbox, representing all ages, genders and continents. The final selection was made based on which stories were able to connect with the part of our mind that anticipates fear and is determined to overcome it. Among the finalists, readers will meet a solo female traveller trying to process her thoughts after a bomb falls near her hotel in Israel, a young rock climber facing the very real prospect of plummeting to his death, and a new mother seeking an answer to her depression during a solo hiking trip. Some stories explore the fear produced when we face a physical threat; others delve into the fear that arises when we realize we aren't exactly sure who we are or who we want to be; others yet seek to explore what exactly drives us to do something for the first time, even if it may be our last.

All of the stories are presented in their original English form. While they have, by necessity, been edited for clarity and readability, all efforts have been made to preserve the voice and intention of the author. In most cases, the writing styles and grammar reflect the home country of the author. Readers will find stories with snippets of foreign languages, preserved to offer insight into the experience of the writer, along with moments of uncertainty that may produce a feeling of disorientation, another glimpse into the reality of travellers and adventure seekers. In some cases, names of characters have been changed to protect the privacy of real people.

We welcome you to *Fearless Footsteps* and the journey on which you are about to embark.

Nathan James Thomas and Jennifer Roberts (editors)
IntrepidTimes.com

Everything is Going to be Okay...

J. D. MARTENS

'Get on your wetsuit, *re*,' Svestis says back to me from the driver's seat, addressing me with familiarity.

About 50 metres from the shore I see it — a little dark speck amid the clear, blue sea. After three nights of staring at a black, spotless sea, the small dinghy floats in between the crests of waves. The dinghy is three large pieces of plywood held up by an inflatable rubber balloon, which wraps around 50 or so refugees inside. It sways back and forth in the wind and buckles inwardly, uncomfortably, as it undulates across the waves.

In the front passenger seat, Alex yanks on his wetsuit with blinding speed. The dinghy hurtles towards the shore, as do we. I quickly jam my foot into the leg hole of my suit as the car jerks violently off the road and onto the rocky beach below. Alex jumps out and hustles to the water, but my foot keeps getting caught on the neoprene of the wetsuit. My heart speeds up and blood jets through my veins as I jam my foot into the leg hole again. I still have my shirt on, my phone in my pocket, and my wallet and my passport ... *shit, where's my passport? ...*

I look up and the dinghy is near. Only Alex is in the water. Svestis is out of the car, too, holding some binoculars and looking for other boats. He looks back at me with a quizzical gaze.

'*Malaka*, what are you waiting for?'

Fuck it!

I leave the suit behind and rush into the sea, slipping on the uneven rocks below. The dinghy is around 30 metres from the shore now, and the brisk Mediterranean water stings like icicles against my skin. Refugees are yelling, pointing, shouting, crying and silent. Those that stand near the edge of the boat lean precariously over its edge.

More guards join us in the water and one yells, '*Sekur al-Motori, Sekur al-Motori.*' Shut off the engine.

But the boat continues unabated into the shallow water. It folds and bends over the waves at the mercy of the sea. Twenty metres. Fifteen.

Finally, one of the people in the back of the boat understands about the engine and pulls the kill line as the water laps against my stomach.

Five metres now. The dinghy dips and bulges like a free-form amoeba. Inside men yell and women cry and children wail and look sickly, shivering even though the day is warm and the sun is pleasant on my skin. I grab the small rope which is attached through little loops on top of the inflatable portion of the dinghy and begin to pull the raft towards the shore.

Arms grab my shoulder as the rope burns my hands and rocks jab into my feet while the boat nears the shore.

'*Shway-shway! Shway-shway!*' I say, trying to smile. Slowly-slowly.

This Arabic phrase effectively means 'calm down', *tranquilo*, everything's going to be alright. The noise and the fear radiate from the boat, and I try to breathe slowly. '*Shway-shway,*' the lifeguards say, '*Shway-shway.*' We say it for ourselves as much as for those in the dinghy, because if people start to jump, the delicate balance of the raft may tip and ...

'*Shway-shway!*' the more involved male refugees start yelling to the women and children.

We pull the dinghy in with the rope. My muscles burn, the water splashes against my face, and I strain with the weight — every wave causes people to lose their balance. Something catches my eye and I glance back towards the boat.

I see a face — a woman directly across from me, staring at me, angry, frightened and overwhelmed.

She grasps in vain at the rope to steady herself. But I need this rope to pull the boat onto the beach. The rope is too far away from her — I'm pulling it away from her — but she grasps desperately for it with her free hand. She's holding a toddler in one arm, and tears stream silently down her face while she grasps helplessly at the rope. She needs it but I can't, and I won't, give it to her. She thrusts her hand absurdly at it, pleading and screaming with her eyes for me to give her the rope, to give her the one thing she can use to keep her balance.

Shway-shway, shway-shway. I smile as best I can.

It'll be over soon, at least this leg of the journey, but her fear and tears are contagious. I've never seen this expression of flight — utter, desperate fear mixed with a sort of unstable relief and a calamitous helplessness. Her disfigured face, angry and despairing and terrified and courageous, her pleading visage for the rope, her eyes, the toddler weighing heavily on her arm. Despite the mayhem and chaos, everything is silent and dimmed, as though it is just me and her, and my mind races from civil war to chemical weapons and from peaceful protests to government authorities with dark rooms and shrouds of black nothingness under roofs of horror.

My eyes start to burn. Her toddler looks around languidly. I force myself to look away from her to focus on the task at hand. The boat is steps away from the shore.

But the woman's face remains. Her brown eyes, the pupils shaking back and forth ever so slightly, the whites of her screaming eyes tinged with red. Her angular jawline and sharp nose, high cheekbones, and two birthmarks just below her left eye. Her tears and her silence. Her little boy, innocent and unknowing, believing his mother when she tells him everything's going to be okay.

Everything is going to be okay, I promise.

I shake my head back and forth to stop myself. Just next to the mother there is a teenager with a hipster haircut, a big grin on his face, and a future in his eyes, ready for the next adventure.

People are trying to jump over me and the other guards into the water. *'Wahid-wahid!'* we yell in atrocious Arabic, pointing to the front of the boat. *One by one.* So the boat doesn't capsize.

The back of the boat still sways with the sea. We are ready for the final pull. I look quickly into the boat, the bottom of which is obscured by dozens of legs and bodies, packed and stacked like poker chips in some sick, ungodly game.

'THREE, TWO, ONE!'

The boat jerks violently forward onto the beach. The crying mother falls down. There is shouting in Arabic. Then more Greek. People are exiting the front of the boat, and it is messy and confusing and dangerous. They slide off the rubber tubes, and the lifeguards catch them before they sink into the water.

The woman hands me her toddler. He is light and has a life vest tied around his neck. I look into the child's eyes and his pupils are dilated wide — he looks directly at me, but his eyes hold no fear, no terror, no emotion at all. He is breathing normally. There are rumours of people giving their children drugs so they don't cry on the journey. If they are too loud, the Turkish Coast Guard might catch the boat, telling them to go back, or worse. Sometimes they try to sink the boats.

I make eye contact with the mother of the child I'm

holding, who is out of the boat now, frantically looking around for her son.

I thought that perhaps we would have another moment — like the one before — a moment of metaphysical understanding, a glimpse of what this woman has been through, but we are far from Hollywood, from nice story arcs and character development and love stories ending in marriage.

I hand the woman her toddler back and she goes to sit down.

There's a man in the middle of the boat who is clutching his chest, unable to walk. I shout to Alex and point. More rapid Greek.

More people start walking off the boat now, and some help the man with chest pain stumble onto the shore. Women hand me wet babies and toddlers, some crying, most silent.

I stand, helpless, as Dr Chelsea tends to the man clutching his heart. She works quickly and purposefully until he is stable. There are girls checking their phones and speaking rapidly.

Finally, the boat is empty. Other volunteers give out blankets to shivering and wet people. There are boxes full of socks and shoes and other dry clothes.

Then, another boat appears in the distance.

'*Pame* Jonah, *Alex! Pame!* Let's go!' Svestis yells from the car.

'Come on, *re*,' Alex says to me, wiping water from his face.

We run over to the car and I hop in the front, Alex gets in the back, and Svestis guns the car into gear, jerking us back onto the paved road. Alex and I keep our eyes on the boat, and I use the binoculars that Svestis brought with him. The boat of refugees — no, of people, dozens of people — bucks with the waves in its fragility above the turbulent waters below. I see so many people.

'It looks like the coast guard will take the ship,' Svestis says and Alex nods.

'What now?' I ask.

'Now is the time for cigarettes!' Alex laughs, and he begins to roll one while Svestis twists and swerves to avoid the potholes in the ground.

I look out at the dinghy, which is now attached to the coast guard vessel, and Alex says something in English, but it doesn't reach me.

'Maybe they are from Sweden?' Svestis says, their voices still distant. 'Blue eyes, blonde hair … They are beautiful, *re*, the new volunteers.'

'What about the people on the shore?' I ask vaguely. 'Are they okay? Shouldn't we help distribute the blankets and food?'

My wetsuit is still in the backseat, unused.

Svestis smiles over at me in the passenger seat, '*Malaka*, our job is to make sure no one dies. We make sure no one drowns in the water, and everyone is stable. Dr Chelsea is dealing with the hypertension patient, so now we wait again. Don't worry, *re*, congrats on your first boat!'

'My first boat ...' I repeat, frowning.

They go back to talking about the girls, and I look back towards the shimmering sea, towards the little inflatable dinghy being pulled by the modern coast guard vessel, my heart pumping quickly, my mouth silent, and my consciousness filled with a face. We didn't even do that much.

Somewhere Over the Rhinogs

EMILY PAYTON

My son was eighteen months old and I was in the grips of depression. Only my husband had picked up on it and seemed determined not just to save me, but to bring back the woman he used to know.

I cried alone all day, and I cried alone all night. I hated being a mother, a wife. I hated my job situation, having to prop up my mother, having to hold my family together with a rapidly unravelling piece of thread. I was trapped in a life I had never wanted but, somehow, had ended up living. And most of all, I hated myself for feeling all those things, because I should have felt lucky. I was lucky.

The guilt ate away at me. I was selfish. I felt disgusted. To make up for it, I did my best to look and act perfect. But eventually, the fragile shell would crack and crumble, and my husband would come home from work and find me crying on the bathroom floor after I had ultimately palmed my son off to my in-laws. I would sob hysterically, unable to stop; unable to stop the whirring in my head, unable to end it all. I would cry until I was exhausted and then I would sleep ... for 100 years it felt. And when I woke, I was still tired and drained, but the liability would drown me. I promised I would get it together, that things would be better. I felt better after letting it out. And so, the cycle continued.

'You love hiking. You love nature,' Matt said cheerfully.

'Wales is a dumbed-down version of Scotland. Let's go somewhere warm, and we'll leave the baby with your parents,' I sneered. I had become cold and cruel in my attempts at controlling myself. 'He's happier with them anyway.' Matt stared out of the front window as we sat in my car. I had dashed out for bread and milk but had been 'gone for hours' apparently. When I pulled up at home, I couldn't bear the thought of going back into the house. I had sat in the car for god knows how long, contemplating how fast I would have to ram the car into the neighbour's wall, so I could be taken to hospital just for something else to feel, something else to focus on.

'We're going tomorrow. Everything is packed.'

'You'll leave me eventually.'

A sigh.

'I'm not. I will never leave you.'

'I'll make you leave me, and you can have the baby. I'll have an affair!' I declared. For a brief moment, he looked like he was going to laugh.

'It's not in you to do that. Stop being so frightened of beating this. Stop being so frightened of *it*.'

*** *** ***

The drive up to North Wales had not been pleasant. The baby hadn't slept well, which meant neither Matt nor I had slept either. I also couldn't understand why nobody had thought it a good idea to build a motorway straight through to North Wales. Why on earth had they kept the twisty, windy roads that just made car sickness inevitable? It was also stiflingly hot, and as we hadn't been able to afford to have the car's air conditioning fixed yet, we had had to open the windows and breathe the 'pure Welsh air' as one old, mad biddy had beamed when we had stopped for a drink. The baby was eventually sick as we passed Bala Lake, and both Matt and I snapped at each other as we disagreed over whose job it had been to pack spare clothes for this situation. Turned out to be my mistake. Like always.

Matt had 'oo-ed' and 'awwwd' over the vibrant green fields, trying to pronounce the place names (which, frankly, just got ridiculous the further north we went), and nearly crashed when he saw a phone box in the village of Trawsfynydd. But we eventually found the log cabin Matt had booked, and after assembling the travel cot, we all fell asleep without taking much notice of it.

Only one word can describe sleeping in a log cabin in North Wales: blackout. Matt and I slowly awoke to hear birds chirping away and hearing their little feet hopping along the roof. It was the first time in a long while that I felt as if I had genuinely been asleep. I didn't jerk awake with dread or with an already chattery mind. I also didn't recall the baby waking. The sun glowed behind the curtains, sending warmth around us as we dozed in and out. Perhaps that Welsh air did have some magic in it. We eventually, lazily, got out of bed and were astonished to find it was gone nine, with the little one showing no signs of stirring. We had always been early risers, even before the baby, so this, for us, was a massive lie-in! We quietly made coffee and sat out on the front veranda with the front door ajar, so we could listen out for wailing. I gazed out at the view in front of me in astonishment.

The Rhinogs, a range of mountains, gazed back at me, looking strong and stable. I noticed Matt watching me — we hadn't spoken really since waking up.

'Why don't you go up them? On your own?' he suggested. I didn't look away.

'You trust me enough to come back then,' I said tonelessly.

✳ ✳ ✳

I had passed the rolling grassy hills of Diffwys and Y Llethr. A faint breeze rustled across them as I looked at the broad ridge, which was lined by a stone wall running along its entire length. My gentle walk had ended. It got tough now.

As I started to climb, I banished any thoughts that attempted to break through. Not thinking was helping, and I found the harder I worked, the easier those thoughts were to dismiss. I was north of Y Llethr, where a sudden change of scenery opened out. I stared emotionlessly at a steep descent leading down to the dark blue Llyn Hywel Lake. I felt unfazed ... steely. I knew it was breathtaking, but I almost felt like tutting. What did this range know? What had it seen compared to me? Beyond, I could see the twin summits of Rhinog Fach and Rhinog Fawr, highlighted by the blue hue of the Irish Sea further still. I continued.

The terrain was tough — it was what I wanted. I needed to get through it. The valley between the two mountains was soft but boggy, with clumps of thick, tufted grass making me work for every footstep. Rhinog Fawr rose up above me. At first glance, it looked threatening, but then it turned into something else. Solidarity and fierceness began to feel safe rather than dangerous. The surrounding nature of the rock and vast openness of the countryside made me feel sturdy. It wasn't trying to defeat me; it was trying to protect me. There were no paths or distinct routes up, just crags where I had to navigate a course over boulders, unstable rocks and gnarly branches of heather which seemed determined to hold me down, to entangle me and keep me from pushing on, but I pulled myself free each time.

The feeling of being all alone in the wilderness after the satisfaction of completing some trying physical exercise was draining, but another sense began to creep in the closer I got to the summit. I was breathing hard when I made it. I was sweating, and millions of midges started to feast on me, but I ignored them. I felt the edges of positive emotion in my heart, the first in such a long time. As I looked, I realized I was humbled. What did I know compared to this mountain range? What had I seen? *Nothing*. Compared to the history and geographical evolution that must have taken place here since the beginning of time, I knew nothing. I felt a surge of being overwhelmed with what I saw and what I had done. I could think clearly for the first time in eighteen months. I saw myself clearly as I could see the silhouettes of the summits. I looked behind to the south Rhinog Fach and Y Llethr, the place I had come from, and saw so much more than just a mountain range. I saw what I had faced, and I felt the negative emotions slightly loosen their grip — I could finally breathe a little easier.

I took a long, deep breath of that magical Welsh air. For the first time in eighteen months, I wasn't frightened of going home. I *wanted* to go home.

They Pay Rent in Paradise

MARIA BETTEGHELLA

The world is divided into two kinds of people: those who enjoy a conversation with a drunk individual, and those who don't. As I hand a third beer to a talkative Turkish guy, I struggle to smile; I clearly belong to the second category. The guy is mumbling something in a strong Middle Eastern accent. The 'honesty of trees' is the focus of his monologue. I usually don't notice when someone is wasted, but if I do, I simply can't stand watching a human being making a show of himself.

I move up and down behind the bar, looking for something to do, but it's only 7:00 p.m. on a rainy Monday. This drunk guy is my only customer and he's not going to let the conversation die. I can't escape, so I end up giving him my opinion, while the look on my face spoils it all. I sincerely believe trees don't lie.

I'm volunteering as a bartender in Mezrab, one of the most

active storytelling houses of Europe, and amongst the few strongholds of Amsterdam underground culture. This cultural centre is managed entirely by an Iranian family and an army of volunteers run story nights at least twice a week. If you happen to have ventured in Amsterdam on your own, this place will resemble a modern Wild West tavern, somewhere to feel safe while an actor or an improvisational comedian lifts your spirit up for a while.

I look into my customer's dark, Turkish eyes. He carries a childish look. He must have been the most annoying kid in the classroom back in the day. There is no sign of intuition in those plain eyes. I grab a beer and start sipping it slowly. I don't understand how a cold beer can possibly match even colder weather, but I keep drinking anyway, and I start saying, 'There are many reasons to travel. For me, it was a poetic quest, a feeling more than a plan. A way to escape, one could say, and yes, I won't deny it.' The beer is still too cold, but the taste is pleasant and it's easier to drink once you've started. 'I'm from Southern Europe.'

'Me too!' the Turkish guy shouts in excitement. He has already told me where he's from, but I simulate a surprised reaction. It helps me to pause, take another sip and reformulate.

'I'm also from the south of Italy,' I continue, 'which means I come from a backwards culture; one that considers me a wife first, and a woman later. Sometimes travelling is the only chance you get to survive.'

My drunken friend is listening carefully, but whether his dark eyes keep still in concentration or perdition, I cannot say.

'I picked New Zealand when I was fifteen years old. I couldn't have found a farther place unless I travelled to Mars.'

'Why did you start travelling?' The Turkish guy is observing me as if my eyes could reveal more of myself than my own words.

'I was scared that if I didn't ... I would end up in a story that wasn't mine. Fear and travel have been the two sides of my life.'

Before turning into an adult, I had already developed a wild eagerness for remote landscapes, different cultures and unfamiliar places. Travelling was therapy — a mirror and an opportunity to cure my deepest fear; fear of being trapped into a life that wasn't mine, playing the role of a daughter that wasn't me and that of a woman that wasn't free. My Turkish customer is as far from home as I am. I'm guessing that, like me, he has also spent enough time away to be unsure of what the word 'home' even means.

Just like third culture kids who grow up removed from their roots, I chose to belong to more than one place. I ended up feeling at home only when I'm on the move. The adrenaline of arriving in a new place is what resembles the feeling of home the most to me.

'We did change a few houses with my family when I was a kid, but no more than three times, and never outside of Italy,' I say, in answer to an earnest question from my Turkish friend. My words hang in the air like the mild wind I remember from the beaches of Brazil.

'Still, I inherited a nomadic lifestyle and that's probably

because it calms the fear. I need to know that moving is always an option for me, otherwise I feel trapped. Travelling is the same door that gets me out every time I need to.'

Now my answer feels a bit more solid, like the Andes that waited for me between Argentina and Bolivia.

'After the exchange in New Zealand, Brazil at 22 was easy. And then Argentina. And then Portugal. Now that I think about it, it's been more than ten years that I have been living in different countries. It feels like Brad Pitt in goddamn Tibet.'

'It was seven years in Tibet, not ten.' My Turkish friend has earned his right to talk and, whatever he needs to say, I am ready to listen.

'This is it. You work, you earn your salary, you live a decent life. As long as you can buy yourself a drink.'

I see his point. He must have one of those office jobs, the ones in which you ring a bell if you sell a promotion. Cages of trained monkeys. He must spend his days like me: 40 hours a week, computer-faced in no natural light. But I'm an outdoor cat and so is my new friend. This is what brings us together tonight and, while I open his fourth beer, I think about the time I walked through the Brazilian jungle for six hours. I hear the monkeys screaming from the trees above, and I keep drinking.

'I found this hot Polish woman on Tinder last week,' the Turkish guy says while laughing hard and I have a flashback of disgust. It's time for another sip, but my beer is empty, so I pour myself a shot of vodka.

'You should see her tits, my Lord!' The Turkish guy is lost in his thoughts and I regret having started this conversation, so I try an emergency move.

'You know what my brother told me last time I saw him?' I need to gain his attention back.

'What?' he asks, while I hope the Polish breasts are fading away.

'That he would beat me just to show me the difference between love and punishment.' Now that I'm drinking vodka, I feel that I've found the right pace of the conversation.

I arrived in Amsterdam in the middle of what is considered summer by the locals. Days were infinite in their timeless light and the sky stayed shiny until 10:00 p.m. The fairytale didn't last long, and dark, early nights started to win over the days at 5:00 p.m. The change has been so abrupt that I can't even say when it happened. Every expat I've talked to has a paranoia about vitamin D deficiency, due to the lack of sunlight, so I ended up buying some too, hoping the supplements would rescue me from a gradually induced biological depression.

I came to the Netherlands because I needed a fresh start. Can you really give yourself a second chance? I don't know, but that's what travelling also promises. Whether life will keep that promise, I guess is a matter of luck.

'Aren't you married?' the Turkish guy asks. He is a fast drinker and I see where this is going.

'One could ...' I stop myself from getting another shot of

vodka only because I need to cycle back to where I live.

'Let me guess, you must have got this beautiful mouth of yours from your mother.' He is already crossing the line, but I have no strength for fighting.

Last time I saw my mother she was screaming. One might have thought she was yelling at me, but the truth is, she was fighting with her younger self, the one who dreamt about travelling but settled instead for an unfair love.

'I am not going to get through this winter.' I ignore the seduction attempt of my customer.

'Yeah? Why not?' he asks. He seems to realize he doesn't have a chance.

'My best friend is from Florida. I'm going to visit her for Christmas and stay there for a while. Start fresh again.' I pour myself some water and prepare to offer my last contribution to this conversation. 'It all looked like social heaven when I first moved here. Then I had to face the renting schizophrenia, the vitamin D paranoia, and this racist attitude floating smoothly around us. It got too hard.'

There are two social groups in Amsterdam: Dutch people and everybody else. You can easily run into a foreigner who has been living in this city for more than twenty years and still doesn't speak a word of Dutch.

'You won't get used to the weather here, but you can live with it.' The Turkish guy is still trying his best, but his voice sounds lower. I wonder if he still remembers the Turkish sun. I feel responsible for his silence, so I quickly add, 'Anyway, the dream faded away quickly for me and it's time to move again. You can't always win, but you can still play another card as long as you are holding some. I guess paradise didn't exist after all.' No tone of regret in my voice, only plain resignation.

'I believe it does,' he says, 'but let me tell you something. I am pretty sure they pay rent in paradise too.'

I look at him, I smile, I nod. His nonsense seems reasonable to me for the first time.

'I'm done for tonight. Don't forget to pay for your three beers, the last one is on me.'

I walk out of Mezrab. Since I last saw my family in Italy, my days have been filled with euphoria and fear. I sat in silence and tried to fill my eyes with the beauty of the world. I wish my mother could be proud of my journey, but I've learnt that I feel her the most when the pain in my chest reminds me that some holes should not be filled. I unlock my bike and off I go, the sun inside and a long road ahead.

A Black Horse

ALANNAH BUCKBY

Framed by the fantastical backdrop of New Zealand's Southern Alps (Kā Tiritiri o te Moana) was a huge black horse. It turned its head to glare, the depthless dark of its mahogany eye a stark contrast to the azure blue sky and silver mountains surrounding it. It was a dream horse, the sort only found in movies or in the pages of a fantasy novel. Its ancient leather saddle creaked as the creature briefly regarded me, but my thrill was hesitant.

The night before we had arrived at a high-country station, lost deep in the mountains of South Canterbury. We had spent many hours driving along a winding dirt road that was rarely found by locals, let alone tourists. The wing-like mountains grew ever bigger around us. When our car got so dusty that we had forgotten what colour it was, we came to the central spine of the Alps — and to a lake that embarrassed the sky with its blueness.

This was our trip of a lifetime, a horse trek in a countryside that few people would ever get to see. The merry but isolated station managers, often bereft of new company, were glad to let us stay in their shearer's quarters. The mammoth 60-kilometre loop through the mountains would be the pinnacle of any horse rider's career.

The following morning produced a perfect dawn. The mountains could be treacherous with their weather but had decided to be kind to us. The autumn wind did not bite, and the first snows were high above, their only purpose was to perfect the view. Our quarters were on a hill, high above the surreal lake. Huge, wooden stockyards for thousands of sheep were laced with corrals and lanes beside them. The view was unreal.

Our guide was an ancient breed of horseman, the sort rare 100 years ago and now nearly extinct in our modern age. This weathered keeper of colonial wisdom could have been anywhere between 40 and 80 years of age. He spoke little and missed even less. Though he would give a stranger the shirt off his back, he disregarded humans but never missed a hair flicker on his beloved horses.

The stockman growled a greeting to us and then immediately interrogated us on our equine experience. He was meticulous and, in turn, led us to the animal he chose. He said he wanted me to ride one of his best horses; he said Coal was a good horse, just a bit hot. Unexpected hesitation welled up inside of me.

The yards were dusty from the long summer and smelled of sheep and pine trees. Clumps of wool were caught here and there on wires and a few pet lambs lounged on the tarnished needles beneath the shelter belt. A few psychotic chickens lurched about. The owners had warned us they had been rescued from a battery farm; redeemed from hell, they now lived in paradise but had never learnt how to 'chicken'. The owners had begged us to be careful when driving in as the chickens did not understand that a tyre could kill them. As they milled about the yards, they clearly did not know that a horse's kick could do the same.

But these were stock horses, solid and quiet. They could work all day on mountainous territory other horses could not go near. They did not waste their energy on batty fowl. The fabulous Coal seemed to hold me in the same esteem as the chickens: irrelevant. I tried to befriend him. Hesitation became doubt and then undeniable fear. I dared not show it, especially not to my mount.

'Just get on, dammit, and you'll never regret it,' I said to myself as I led the massive horse over to the block and mounted. I immediately felt its raw strength under me, half a ton of solid muscle and it was electrified. The imperious creature pranced sideways and made a small buck. I suggested to Coal that he stand still, but he ignored me, so I told him again gently and he abruptly planted his legs but snorted with fury: hmm, opinionated.

Everybody stared at us, marvelling. They said I looked amazing, with beautiful horsemanship. Every compliment was in stark contrast to what I actually felt. I was terrified! If this magnificent brute picked a fight, I would lose and badly.

'He might throw a few bucks,' our guide said, watching, 'then he'll be right.'

I told myself I was fine. I was a good rider and a few bucks were not a bother. I tried to ignore the other buzzing commentary in my head: *But you're not young anymore; help's a long way away if you fall ...*

A few minutes later, Coal threw a few bucks.

We had barely left the yards before a volcanic tantrum unleashed. Coal stormed and shunted another horse out of the way. I cried out to our guide, but he was already far behind as Coal took off in full gallop along the track towards the lake. I tried to stop him, but he had caught the iron bit in his mouth, biting down on it. I used all the strength I had to haul him in, but I might as well have been a flea on his back. I had never been so helpless on a horse.

Up ahead, the track went off a very steep drop as it wound down to the lake. A full gallop down that stony incline was certain disaster. I hauled Coal sideways into a high bank, hoping to slow him down, and he went straight up the 2-metre cutting effortlessly. Now, like a bad Hollywood movie, right before us was a full-wire fence and beyond that a cliff. Coal went straight at it.

I can jump that high fence, I thought through my horror. *I've got this!*

At the last instant, Coal spun. To this day I have no idea how a horse of his size and speed could turn so sharply. He vanished from underneath me. As everyone who gets on a horse should know, I began to roll in mid-air and continued to roll on impact, the only way to reduce injury. I landed hard and then kept rolling until I hit a fence post.

I stayed very still. Moving suddenly is not smart after a fall.

I stared at my camera hanging on a wire above me. It had flown off my shoulder, never touching the ground, its strap hooked in the wires; it was now slowly spinning to a halt. Outstanding ... something went right.

I was glad to have survived the fall, although I knew shame would follow. Fear continued to plague me as I sat in the auburn tussock waiting for the others to catch up. *Was I injured? Had I failed? Had I ruined the entire holiday?*

The old stockman was silent as the others fussed over me. He rounded up Coal, and I was certain he was annoyed with me. The others asked if I could continue. Whether it was stupidity or determination to overcome my fear, I answered yes.

'I'll get another horse,' he said, and Coal was towed away. 'You lot go ahead. We'll catch up.'

The others continued down to the lake, and again I was left sitting in the tussock questioning my choices. The stockman returned with a huge red mare with a flowing black mane. She had none of Coal's beauty, presence or fire.

'A good horse?' I asked meekly.

'My best horse,' he huffed back.

This shocked me immensely. I was certain he disliked me. But his currency was grit and mine had somehow impressed him. My legs shook violently as I tried to remount. I tried six times with victory on the seventh. I'd had enough of this fear nonsense. I wanted to ride. As I settled into the new saddle, the stockman touched the boat-shaped star on my new mare's forehead, 'Now Copper, you look after her.'

And Copper did.

Now truly on the best horse I would ever ride, we left our dusty hoofprints and headed into the glorious silver mountains and toward adventure. Copper was the most loving horse I'd ever met. She was close to human in her intelligence, as if she'd understood what her owner had said. She never left my side, following me like a dog unbidden. She carried me over ethereal mountains, down scree slopes and through boulder-ridden ravines. Crystal snowmelt rivers rushed pearlescent beneath her belly, but her only care was for her rider. I've never bonded as quickly or as deeply with anyone or anything as I did with that glorious mare.

I have now travelled and ridden all over the world, but nothing has ever compared to that majestic trek. I had bruising the full length of my body, and it was painful the entire ride, but I never came to regret any moment of it.

Always get back on.

The River

ROSLYN JOLLY

The water looked so inviting.

We had spent the early morning in the rainforest, setting off in the dark so we could catch the dawn breaking over the mist-wreathed canopy. It was hot, sticky walking that included climbing a thousand steps up a series of stairways and ladders built to take visitors to the very top of the trees, where we could see eye to eye with the birds and gibbons. Although it was an elating experience, it had left us sweat-soaked and leg-sore.

Now, back at our base — a guesthouse deep in Ulu Temburong National Park — we had a choice: shower, don fresh clothes, and spend the rest of the morning on the veranda with a good book; or cool off by tubing down the Temburong River.

The first option fit my natural outlook on life. It's the option I'd choose in a personality test. 'You have just completed a challenging trek through a remote rainforest in high heat and humidity. Do you (a) relax in the shade with a cool drink, or (b) embark on another physical challenge that you are even less equipped to perform than the first one.' Duh!

But, as I said, in its own way, the water looked inviting.

Surveying the other members of our group, I reckoned I had ten years on the oldest of them. Plus, they all seemed to know what 'tubing' was and how to do it. I had to have the concept explained to me. It *sounded* simple enough, but ...

I know nothing about rivers. I grew up on the coast, and to me the ocean is the natural medium for swimming. It's salty and sandy and clean and sparkly and, above all, blue. Also, if you follow some basic rules, you can always get out of it. Rivers are not blue, and you can't see what's happening beneath the surface of them, on their unimaginable, muddy bottoms. So why would I here, so far from home, surrounded by strangers, entrust myself to this greeny-brown alien thing snaking through the jungle?

And yet, it would be wet and cool, and the very cells of my body longed to feel its perhaps treacherous embrace.

'I don't know,' I said doubtfully to our guide, a local man in his twenties. 'I feel like there's a lot that could go wrong.' The guide assured me that I'd be fine, that anyone could do it. He brushed aside my objection that I didn't know how to steer the rubber ring that would carry me down the river. 'I'll show you once we're in the water.'

With that, he jumped into his own tube and the current whisked him away. Most of the rest of the group had already set off, and the last few were joining them. It was a moment of decision: stay on shore in what was definitely my comfort zone, or step into the river and thereby into the unknown.

I stepped into the river, backed into my rubber ring and let go of the shore.

The first few minutes were pure bliss. The water delivered the most satisfying feeling of refreshment I have ever known. It was cool in a way that had nothing to do with coldness — there was no icy edge, no underlying chill, just a soft caressing lowering of temperature that soothed the skin and calmed the mind. Cradled in my tube, partly immersed as I floated downstream, surrounded by the silent forest, I thought of the poet Andrew Marvell's line, 'a green thought in a green shade'. Delightful!

The first sign of trouble was the appearance, mid-river, of a tangle of prickly branches piercing the surface, which seemed like a good thing to avoid.

'How do I ... ?' But the guide was far out of earshot, as were all my fellow tourists.

It now became apparent that the current was stronger than I'd realized and was carrying me straight towards the protruding branch-islet. I managed to reach out a hand and push off from the obstacle, but that sent me irretrievably careening towards the other side of the river and away from the shore I was meant to be aiming for.

I could see the funny side of this; a somewhat round, very white, middle-aged woman was spinning wildly in a rubber ring on a river in the middle of a forest in the middle of Borneo, a place whose name has given us a term that's a synonym for remoteness: 'the wilds of Borneo'. There was also a not-quite-so-funny side. I was trying to navigate a fast-flowing current in a contraption I had no idea how to manage because the guide who had promised to show me how had vanished and left me to my own devices.

It wasn't hard to see that this might not end well. The rest of the group had now reached our agreed destination, a point where a smaller creek branched off from the river, but I was still sailing merrily, merrily down the stream with absolutely no control over my journey.

Never has the proposition that life is but a dream seemed so plausible as during the next few seconds as the others became diminishing figures on a receding shore.

'Don't worry, Roslyn! I'll get you!' It wasn't the guide yelling this but one of the other tourists who plunged back into the river. I'd only met her three days previously, but there she was, Kate-my-mate, a fearless friend, half my age and twice as gutsy, freestyling strongly through the current, coming to catch me and tow me to shore.

It was a glorious rescue. It had verve and daring, and I love the fact that my rescuer was a young woman. We reached the shore unscathed, where Kate was rightly hailed as the hero of the day.

If this story has a moral, I don't know what it is. Know your limits? Act your age? Remember that if something can go wrong, it probably will? Beware of disappearing guides? Or, seize the day, go with the flow, love the world and, in some way, it will love you back? Take your pick.

The water had been inviting and I had accepted the invitation. The river had a few tricks up its sleeve, but I was lucky — someone kind and brave had been there to help. Would I do it again? Well, they say you can't step into the same river twice. But I'll never forget the touch of that cool water or the feeling of being, just for a few minutes, connected to an environment so alien and beautiful.

The Rust Sanctuary

DARMON RICHTER

In Athens, the streets smelled of bread. It was a hot July and tourists thronged the Acropolis, cats begged noisily at tables in outdoor restaurants, the streets choked with taxis and every market vendor spoke just enough English to harass the crowds with shiny trinkets and ice-cold bottles of Coke. It's amazing how fast Greece changes, however, when one leaves the capital behind. Five hours south we travelled, down a coastline that alternated from picturesque beaches to shipwrecks and oil refineries. We shared a train carriage with villagers and an Orthodox priest in full black robes, who smelled of sweat and incense. When we ran out of serviceable track, we took a bus the rest of the way.

Somewhere along the highway, the police pulled us over. Two officers entered the bus, lumbered past us down the aisle, then escorted a pair of boys from their seats, out to the roadside. These boys had dark skin, hardly any luggage, and, from the sign-language pantomime they performed beside the police car under the cypresses, it seemed they didn't speak a single word of Greek. 'Syrians,' someone whispered, and then the bus continued on south without them.

We reached Patras, Greece's third-largest city, just as it was getting dark. The streets here were narrower, free from the tourist hordes of Athens, and busy instead with the mosquito-whine of mopeds. The local city beaches weren't the best, we were told; too small and too crowded. So, the next day we followed a tip and went looking for a scenic spot further down the coast. That's when we saw it — the old paper mill sitting beside the road out of the city. A citadel of rust and barbed wire reared up behind a security fence, the building's plaster façade baked to a dirty orange by the sun. The factory looked ominously out of place on this sea-front strip; a hulking shadow of a former industrial age, with the promise of deeper, darker shadows within. As if magnetized, immediately we knew we had to see inside.

There was a police patrol car parked on the road to the factory yard. 'Look like you belong here,' my Greek friend said. 'Don't make eye contact.' The car was faced down the road away from us as we walked quickly past — heads down, avoiding eye contact. Through the gate ahead of us, the dead factory loomed, and we slipped out of sight from the road, scampering inside and melting into its foreboding embrace. All the while, the police didn't once budge from their post; we didn't yet know that they were here for someone else.

When the old paper mill died almost 30 years ago, it left behind a colourful corpse. Red rust residue bled down yellowed walls, meeting the green creepers and leaves that burst up from below. Waxy Mediterranean vegetation tore its way through the old concrete plaza. The first building we passed was little more than a roofless hall where sunlight sliced through broken machinery: beams and rafters, winches and gears, the guts of the old factory left open to the burning sky. What remained of the ceiling looked fit to fall at any moment. The next building was larger though, hard-edged and formidable. Its steel and concrete skeleton was broken only by windows of thick orange glass, grown fuzzy with cobwebs, and just a single tear across the wall, where the bricks parted like an open wound to reveal an inky blackness within. Our curiosity won. Checking to make sure no one had seen us, we focused on our courage and stepped hastily into the void.

Inside the gloom, a steady drip of water kept time, a metronome for a place that time had otherwise abandoned. In that first hall, archaic pipes, valves and canisters lined the back wall. A heavy winch hung dead from its chain, machinery whose purpose had long since been forgotten. Deeper into the bowels of the factory we went, following a trail of corruption — broken bottles, soiled newspapers, ceramic machine parts and coils of rusted wire that clutched lifelessly at our boots. We turned a corner and I think I must have gasped out loud to see the space beyond — a darkened tunnel extended ahead, its floor flooded in pooling water that reflected every concrete pillar to give the illusion of a grand, high-ceilinged gallery fit for a temple, while at the far end, light burst in through a busted roof to illuminate white pillars tangled in a shock of green growth. We passed through the darkness of the cloister into light, to this strange garden, where old industry had been transformed by a chaos of life and health. That's when the ruin's residents found us.

The first sign was voices. We heard them outside the walls, coming around the back side of the factory. We listened and waited ... the voices stopped and we could breathe again for a moment, but then a metal clang rang out in the neighbouring hall and my friend said, 'They're inside.'

I peered around the corner, looking down the empty factory hall. Framed in the light at the entrance were three figures, all lithe, muscular and heading our way. It was too late to hide, we'd been seen already. One of them whistled as they walked towards us, a series of discordant notes that bounced about the empty factory space. We stood stock-still. I felt my hand tighten around the shaft of my camera tripod. Suddenly another whistle took up the call, the sound drifting down from above. With a heavy feeling, I cast my gaze up to see bodies moving in the rafters. Then another figure broke from a pillar, high up on the far wall, walking the ledge that circled the factory floor. There were voices behind us now, too, and I guessed there were eight of them, at least. Maybe more ... maybe *many* more.

I braced myself as the three strangers closed in, and then they stepped out of the shadows before us and, in the soft light of the garden hall, we saw that they were only in their teens or early twenties, at most. For a few awkward moments, we simply looked at each other until suddenly, the first stepped forward and quickly shook hands with each of us. 'Hello,' he said, though they continued to eye us with caution; it seemed clear that they were living here and that we'd wandered straight into their sanctuary. We asked where they were from, and they told us Afghanistan. 'How is it there right now?' my friend asked. 'Not good,' came the reply.

Above us, in the rafters, the others listened in on this exchange. As my eyes got used to the shadows, I made out more faces peering down from the metal beams and the corner of a sleeping bag, dangling over the edge. In another corner of the hall, a basic clothesline was strung up with socks and shirts.

Only one of these young men seemed to understand English, and we asked him how long he'd been here in the factory. 'I arrived today,' he said. He had the youngest looking face of the three but a beard that would have made an ageing lumberjack proud. Some of the others, he told us, had been here for over a year. They wanted to go to Italy, he said — the ferry sails six times a week from Patras to Bari — and their plan was to hitch a ride, stow away somehow, and maybe find a better life at the other end.

We all shook hands again before we left. I said good luck to each of them ... although really, the words felt hollow. It wasn't luck that had got them here, but rather, bad luck that had driven them out of their home country, and then courage and perseverance to see it through. I thought about my own luck in comparison — a good passport, a credit card and family, who'd probably mortgage a house if my life ever really, truly, depended on it. I will likely never experience the kind of fear these travellers had already overcome, and I realized then that sometimes the illusion of courage is itself a luxury.

On the way out of the paper mill, I noticed a sign pinned to the fence in English: *Approach is Strictly Forbidden. The Buildings are Uninhabitable and Dangerous.* Beside that was the same message printed in Arabic script.

The Art of Speaking Fearlessly

RACHAEL ROWE

A plume of acrid cigarette smoke stung my eyes as the senior nurse glared at me in contempt while exhaling on her Gitane. Her makeup was plastered to her face, giving her the appearance of a porcelain doll. She had immaculately manicured nails that circled her cigarette. These hands were clearly not designed for hard work in a busy surgical ward. I stared as her mouth opened to speak.

'*Je déteste les Anglais.*' 'I hate English people.'

This was not the welcome I had expected on my first day in a Swiss hospital. The opportunity to work in a French-speaking environment with the added bonus of travel seemed like a dream job when I applied for the post. I had passed a strict entrance exam in written and spoken French with a pass rate of 80 per cent to be able to work here, but with this woman in charge, that counted for nothing. What was I going to do? I had dreamed of working overseas and travelling, but it now appeared to be a fantasy.

Determined to succeed, I persevered with my decision to work in a French-speaking setting. Each day brought a new challenge to overcome. Although I spoke French and could understand much of the conversations, it took just one mispronounced word or hesitation to provoke criticism from Suzanne, the nurse in charge. To make matters worse, when I hesitated before speaking, it was assumed I knew nothing at all. At that time, British nurses were not trained to put up a drip or intravenous infusion, which meant I had to be trained in this skill. This brought further sighs of contempt from Suzanne. It became hard to say anything at all, and I was fearful for my livelihood and the shame of returning home as a failure.

However, there were lighter moments too. One day I spent all afternoon trying to understand one elderly lady, only to discover that she herself was muddling her words and hadn't been making much sense at all, much to the amusement of the staff. And then there were the drunk people whose slurred speech became a real challenge to understand in French. My nemesis was the ward round where several people would be talking at once, making it hard to focus on one person when trying to comprehend French. How was I going to overcome these difficulties in understanding the language?

I lived for my days off when I could escape from the sneers of the senior nurse. Each day I planned a new adventure — hiking in the Swiss Alps, exploring beautiful parts of Switzerland, and taking the train to other parts of Europe.

I made the most of every moment, enjoying views of the Matterhorn, walking in the Bernese Oberland, and taking in the peace of an alpine meadow. The staff at the railway station began to recognize me, bemused at this young English woman exploring the country by train. In fact, it was these friendly conversations that made me realize that I was able to communicate effectively and could succeed in this job. It was as though there was an invisible barrier to speaking another language, which required determination to be able to break through and succeed. It required a fearlessness of sounding stupid, not being afraid to experiment and being able to make the odd mistake. And that took courage.

My opportunities to overcome these difficulties came quite unexpectedly. One night, I was on duty caring for a very sick lady. Her relatives were staying with her. I offered them a cup of tea and they seemed delighted and thrilled to be served tea by an English nurse, although the circumstances were very sad. At the time I thought nothing of it, but those relatives spoke to the head of the department the following morning about how kind I had been to them, and the message got back to the senior nurse. Just that small act of compassion made Suzanne begin to realize that, although I came from another country, I was a nurse at heart. Now I could aim higher with my language skills.

My next challenge was the ward round and the professor. Ward rounds were known as 'la Grande visite', which summed up the attitude and culture perfectly. They were hierarchical and very formal, but anyone on the round needed to understand the orders being given. That required concentration and was difficult when everyone was talking simultaneously. When the professor's entourage swept into the department, I knew that if I got this wrong there would be trouble. As usual, all the doctors were talking at once over the patient, each trying to impress the professor. Somewhere in the debate instructions were issued. As the professor turned to go to the next patient, I stood in front of him, smiled and politely asked, 'Before you see the next patient, can I just check I have your instructions written correctly?'

There was a gasp from one of the other nurses as no one ever spoke to the professors like that. In fact, nurses were not supposed to speak on a ward round at all. The junior doctors looked in astonishment. But today was different. The professor paused, smiled and ensured I had all the orders written down correctly. This continued for the rest of the round as he summarized his instructions to make sure the orders were accurate, and his patients were getting the care they needed. It also helped the patients understand what was happening. I waited for a reprimand from the senior nurse, but it never came. Instead, one of the surgeons walked up to me later that day and said, 'You are very brave to come here and work in a different language. It's not easy.'

By now I felt bold enough to go further with my language skills. I felt as though I was breaking through this invisible barrier of fear when speaking French or not quite understanding something. This time I wanted to tackle attitudes and behaviours around the nursing care.

I had taken the handover of a patient deemed aggressive by the staff. He had fractured his pelvis and was physically restrained due to his apparent confusion about where he was and what was happening around him. I introduced myself to him and asked him how he was feeling. He turned to look at me and tried to say something, but the words weren't coming out. I could see it irritated him.

'Take your time.'

Again, he tried to say something. But what? He was frustrated.

'Try again. I don't mind if you speak slowly. It helps me understand you.'

This time he managed one word and looked at the wall. I took his hand in mine and said, 'You're not confused, are you?'

He stared at me. His eyes looked imploringly into mine. In that silence there was a shared understanding.

'Squeeze my hand if you are finding it difficult to say something.' He squeezed my hand. I asked him to do the same with his other hand. That was significantly weaker. Suddenly I realized what had happened. This man had suffered a stroke, which had affected his speech. I called the doctor over and explained what I believed to be happening. Initially, he looked bemused and was not impressed to be asked to do something, especially by an English nurse. When he reluctantly went to see the man, he soon realized I had a point. The man's difficulty in expressing himself was causing him to be angry. His fracture had been prioritized, but the stroke needed urgent treatment. We were able to transfer the man to a specialist stroke unit. In that moment the patient and I had a shared recognition of the difficulties of not being understood.

A few weeks later, I was writing up reports when I noticed the professor had come into the department. He asked if he could speak to me. Expecting trouble, I followed him into the nearby office.

'Your French is so much better now,' he said. 'In fact, I would like to ask a favour of you.'

What could he possibly want?

'I have a very important presentation to do in California next month. Could you please proofread my work and ensure the English is perfect?' Even he needed help at times.

Being able to speak languages enables us to communicate on a wider level and with people we would not otherwise encounter. There is an art to being able to speak fearlessly, and when we have broken through those barriers of sounding strange and not knowing a word or two, a whole world opens up before us.

Dirty Feet in Taipei

KATE MOXHAY

The receptionist gestured towards the pink swimsuit poking out of my backpack and gave a stern shake of her head. 'No, madam. You swim, everything go off!' She pointed to a small sign on the desk stating as much, and I immediately regretted neglecting to check this small but vital detail before I arrived. I must have looked slightly startled then, suddenly paler perhaps. 'Absolutely everything? Even knickers?' I asked. She looked at me patiently, an expression of puzzlement on her face. 'Well, obviously' it seemed to say.

I was in Beitou, a peaceful, forested suburb of Taipei, famous for its steaming mineral springs and bathhouses. I was travelling alone on a short trip away from Manila, eager to escape the hectic, traffic-choked streets of my new home and keen to experience one of Taiwan's most popular pastimes. Standing at the entrance to one of the oldest bathhouses in the area, red-faced and sweating from the summer heat, I was ready for a swim and a bit of cultural immersion — quite literally. Instead, I found myself cursing my delicate English sensibilities.

To bathe completely naked in a Taiwanese bathhouse is, of course, completely normal. Considered more hygienic than swimwear, it's also thought to be more relaxing and therapeutic to cast all clothing asunder — a concept I was yet to grasp. Similarities between the bathhouses of Beitou and the Japanese *onsen* are obvious. The springs themselves have always been here, bubbling up their steamy waters from Taiwan's geologically heated depths, but they were only fully utilised after the Japanese began their occupation of Taiwan back in 1895. Soldiers saw the potential of the area as a place for rest and relaxation and began to build bathhouses in the traditional style, with wooden floors, stone walls and partially open to the elements. They came to relax and soak up the mineral goodness, as well as alleviate feelings of homesickness.

Kawayu Hot Spring, where I now stood, is set high up on a densely forested hill, where myriad calls of local birds fill the humid air and the streets are blissfully free of traffic. The entrance is neatly hidden with just a small gate and a quietly bubbling stream tumbling down alongside a long set of steep stone steps hinting at its existence. It looked like the entrance to a secret world, and I couldn't wait to step inside. I had eschewed the public hot spring bath (too busy) and the plush five-star resorts down the hill (too expensive). I was after the real deal ... or so I'd thought.

So now here I was. It was everything I'd been searching

for, but, rather naïvely, I hadn't counted on the full monty. I pleaded again with the receptionist, who was polite but unmoving. 'Maybe just the knickers?' The head shaking resumed. So, I hired a tiny rough towel, grabbed a plastic shower cap from the pile on the desk and headed through crisp white linen curtains into the changing area.

A small neat room greeted me with lockers on one side and the usual hair drying apparatus and mirrors on the other, as well as a collection of tiny plastic stools. It was clean, functional and busy. I'd removed my sandals outside, and the stone floor was cool and rough against my feet. I could see the baths just through the door, steaming and welcoming. I clutched my tiny towel and stripped off, careful not to make any eye contact with anyone and stepped tentatively into the bathing area.

The bathhouse was busy with throngs of local ladies, some chatting and giggling in small groups and others just quietly bathing in the pools, eyes closed and zoned out. The air was humid and heavy with sulphur, bright sunlight shone through the slats in the roof and maple trees and sky appeared in the larger gaps. Rather less pleasing was realizing there would be a soundtrack to this otherwise serene experience — speakers hidden in the corners of the roof blasted out classic 1980s tunes, and it wasn't long before I was nervously humming along to Wham's *Wake Me Up Before You Go-Go* while scurrying towards my first dip.

There were three pools to choose from, each with their own therapeutic properties. The sulphur spring looked almost like milk, a result of the stream absorbing volcanic gases on its way through the rock, and it was not too hot but more like a tepid bath. It's believed to help open the lungs and alleviate bronchitis and other lung ailments. The mineral spring, on the other hand, steamed with hot, clear water which smelled faintly of iron. This was the one for aching joints and arthritis sufferers. But the one I really wanted to take a dip in was the radium spring. With tiny traces of radium, this particular kind of spring is found in few places outside of Beitou in Taiwan. It has a greenish tint but is mostly clear and naturally slightly radioactive with properties known to help joints and muscles. I don't know why this one appealed to me the most, but maybe it was the realization that this would probably be the only chance I'd have to immerse myself naked in radioactive waters while simultaneously listening to Wham. Who knows?

I tentatively dipped in my toe; the water was fresh and clear, and I plunged in, my breath caught with the freezing temperature. It was utterly lovely. I sat shoulder deep next to a couple of ladies deep in conversation and tilted my head back to watch the sunlight dapple the wooden roof. It felt wonderful, and I immediately understood why the Japanese, and now the Taiwanese, were so taken with the experience. I looked around and was struck by how sociable the place was. Almost everyone sat in a group or in pairs, and most were elderly and completely uninhibited, talking and laughing. There was a small queue for a series of powerful, steaming showers that pummelled water onto your back at top speed, like the massage setting on a shower turned to hyper speed. A series of wooden stools faced a low shelf filled with shampoo bottles and soap.

I started to feel numb in the freezing radioactive water and headed next to the milky sulphur pool to warm up, then finally heating up to boiling point in the mineral bath. I was starting to relax, forgetting I was the only westerner there and naked to boot.

I was one of the crowd, a bathing pro who knew her minerals from her radium and everything in between. It was at this point, full of confidence and moving casually between pools, almost swaggering, when a woman suddenly approached me. She began insistently pointing at my feet, speaking in fast, urgent Cantonese — and she didn't look happy. Taken aback, I started to laugh nervously and replied, 'Ha! Yes, my feet!' She continued to berate me, and I now noticed people had stopped their conversations and were turning to look at the unfolding drama. I was mortified. There was definitely something wrong with my feet, but I just couldn't work it out. The woman was shouting now, pointing to each pool in turn, then back to me and my terrible feet. It was only after she picked up one of the small buckets sitting at the side of each pool, which up until now I hadn't paid the slightest bit of attention to and began filling it with water and splashing it onto my left foot that I realized I had been walking around brazenly barefooted, smothering my feet with floor grime in the process and then hopping into the pure waters, bringing my feet and all their impure dirt with them. This was, understandably, a grave mistake.

'Ah-ha!' I cried, over both her raised voice and Cyndi Lauper playing in the background and began rinsing my feet hurriedly over and over. She mercifully calmed down, nodded at me and walked away, no doubt content in the knowledge that the pure waters would no longer be sabotaged by this ignorant newcomer.

After the feet fracas my newly found confidence diminished somewhat, and I spent the last 10 minutes chin deep in the radium. But despite the momentary drama, I looked around and understood why this was such a popular pastime. Social, healthy and at once invigorating and relaxing — the humble bathhouse had it all.

Once back out in the bright sunshine, bathed and clothed, I headed straight to a local bar and ordered an enormous beer. I drank it down quickly, its cold bitterness stinging my mouth as I gazed out at the valley, steaming and green. I was proud, a little embarrassed, yes, but for once I felt a little bit less like a tourist and more like a local. My feet were impeccably clean, and I was ready for my next Taiwanese adventure.

Travels with Anxiety

DEVYANI NIGHOSKAR

One Tuesday afternoon in Mirissa, a small tourist town in the south of Sri Lanka, I slouched my sandy self on a beach chair, gazing at the clear blue ocean in front of me. It was a bright, sunny day. However, that was not how I felt. The waves were calm and gentle, yet uncomfortable thoughts raged in my head. As travellers swam in the infinite depths of the ocean, I clutched on to my phone. Texting a friend back home, I told him what a great time I was having in Sri Lanka, on my first solo trip abroad. I lied to him, realizing that I could no longer lie to myself.

'Is it okay if I leave my bag here, while I swim?' I asked a server in a nearby restaurant, trusting him with my money, phone and passport. He nodded and off I ran into the turquoise water. As I swam deeper into the ocean, I suddenly became aware of every moment that I was living. Every wave that gently caressed my body, every thrust that I moved ahead with, every breath I took on the surface, and every thought I had, pointed towards one troubling question — 'Why was I hating my own company?'

The answer is never a simple one. It wasn't supposed to be. I had always believed travelling had the power to heal anyone; that one could always find the answers they were seeking. But sometimes it also posed uncomfortable questions that one may have subconsciously ignored for too long. Perhaps that is why I had landed up in this splendid island country, after facing a professional downfall and a diagnosis of GAD (generalized anxiety disorder), which I had been successfully battling through therapy. But wandering alone through a foreign land with uncertainty and seeking inspiration from the simplest of things was a therapy of its own kind.

So was that swim. It was calming and liberating, but only temporarily. As I found my feet back on the land, I found the anxiety back in mind. Were my belongings safe, was I looking fat in my beach wear, was I going to be alone through the night? The answers to all of the above were in the affirmative.

That night, as I sat by myself anxiously, after a failed attempt of feeling better at a trance dance party and making conversation with others, Firuz who ran the Going Om Hostel, where I was staying, came and smiled at me warmly. 'Why do you travel?' he asked. Surprised at this sudden question I replied almost instantaneously that, 'I travel to learn and unlearn, but I also travel to run away.'

Nothing more needed to be said. He understood what I

was feeling and told me about his own battle with mental health that almost led him to take his life at seventeen. When that attempt failed, Firuz began to travel, thinking that he had nothing more to lose. How he found himself and the hostel through that is a story that only he can do justice to, but he made me realize that it was okay to feel whatever I was feeling. It was okay to embrace my demons and take time to decide what to do next. All is good as long as we carry love in our heart for others and, most importantly, ourselves. He then directed me to look into the mirror the next day and tell myself with love, that I am doing great and that I love myself.

I did what I was told. That simple act didn't solve all my issues. I didn't expect it to, but it certainly gave me the courage to go on with a smile on my face as big as his.

The next morning, I left on a local bus for Galle, a beautiful, erstwhile Dutch heritage town on the coast. Through the window, I gazed at the turquoise ocean, glistening under the afternoon sun, sprawling towards infinity as the waves came crashing over dense hillocks. The coconut trees swayed in the gentle breeze. Sri Lanka's southern province is truly beautiful, but recounting my experiences of the past few days, I realized that its people were even more so.

For shy and socially awkward people like me, who do not particularly understand and enjoy the glamour of solo travel, it was the Sri Lankans that I met who truly helped me battle my fear of loneliness and utter confusion for the ten days I was there. They are the warmest and friendliest people I have ever met.

There was Firuz who had taught me to be comfortable with

my own thoughts. There was Lalina aunty, the caretaker of my hostel at Hikkaduwa, who had looked after me as her own daughter and made sure I was always well fed. Then there was London, my snorkelling instructor who, while on a walk on the beach, told me to seize the moment and have all the fun I could. He later took me to a party where I really put his advice into action. Then there was the kind man at a photo gallery displaying images from the horrific 2004 tsunami, a survivor himself, who tied a holy Buddhist thread around my wrist and prayed for my well-being. While spending time with all these people had acted towards the betterment of my mental health, it was one woman, named Kamani D'Silva, who truly changed my perspective towards fear and life.

Sri Lanka's coast was one of the worst hit by the 2004 tsunami, and its stories still linger in the community. Some of these make it to the museum Kamani D'Silva opened in her house — the same house she lost during the disaster. 'When I saw the first wave, I thought this was the end of the world. Everyone was out running on the streets. After the first wave, a few people went back to grab their belongings, thinking it was over. Then came the second wave. Hardly anyone survived. We didn't return until we were told it was safe. When we came back, only the floor of our house remained. Everything was gone.'

D'Silva did not bother about her ruined material possessions. All she cared about was that her immediate family was safe. She lost a lot of friends and neighbours and rebuilt her house and her life for the next three years. Once things returned to normal, she opened the Community Tsunami Museum where survivors share their stories. From sketches by children to pictures and statistics, from memoirs by tourists who lost their loved ones to deeper realizations of valuing not just our lives but also nature, all find their way in this space. But one also finds courage and inspiration here, especially through Kamani who relives the tragic day, every day as she guides visitors through the museum. 'We never know what will happen, when another wave will eat us up, so we try to make the best of every moment — no grudges and no sadness,' D'Silva says.

* * *

'Madam, Galle is here,' the conductor said, snapping me out of my thoughts. As I took my bag and stepped out of the bus, my head was still buzzing with thoughts of D'Silva. She was right. Life was uncertain. I had to seize the moment and enjoy all that Galle had to offer.

First built by the Portuguese in the late 1500s, Galle was excessively fortified by the Dutch when they took over. The city has museums, churches, temples, mosques, quaint roadside cafés, old Dutch bungalows and quiet lanes all built within the fort that looms over the magnificent ocean. Here I hired a local tuktuk, whose driver became my personal guide and showed me around the entire city and even decided to take me to Koggala, a beautiful, quaint fishing village nearby. There, I spent some time with the fishermen, understanding their lives and livelihoods in great detail, sharing a meal of kottu (a local delicacy, a mishmash of chopped up bread, vegetables, meat and cheese). It was delectable, cheap and wholesome.

At night, I interacted with people from all over the world in my hostel, getting a peep into their lives — and sharing my own stories with them. I also wrote extensively in my journal about my thoughts of the people I was meeting and the experiences I was having. Anxiety often results in you overthinking, which is why you tend to bury yourself in work or distract yourself when you are in your own environment. But when you are out of your comfort zone, on your own, there's little you can do to avoid your thoughts. It is almost as if you are forced to think about what you have been avoiding for so long. This can be terrifying, especially when a part of you so badly wants to enjoy and immerse yourself in the rich culture that the destination has to offer. But it is also imperative and somewhat inevitable.

Sri Lanka is beautiful and so am I, in more ways than one. I did not find my answers in the end, but I knew what my questions were. I had finally faced my demons. Now to do defeat them, perhaps I need another solo trip? Vietnam, maybe?

Playing with Blue Fire

NIAMH DOHERTY

I lay on the bed with my heavy eyes battling the illuminated terracotta curtains. It was only 6:00 p.m., but it was time to sleep. Our bags sat next to us, packed as if we were in some way 'prepared' for the night ahead. The hot Javan sun beamed into the room, cancelling out the redundant aircon and making it impossible to sleep. We were both physically exhausted from our early rise at midnight and equally as exhausted at the thought of setting our alarms for another midnight waking. We had conquered Mount Bromo the night before and lowered ourselves through the flowing waters of Tumpak Sewu the day before that, but I couldn't help but feel uneasy about Mount Ijen.

I rolled over to see my boyfriend Tommy reading and scrolling through online reviews. I began to do the same, but the TripAdvisor reviews only fuelled my ever-growing fear: 'Hardcore, but worth it', 'Six-km roundtrip steep hike to crater's edge', 'Be prepared for an uphill trek', 'Not worth the risk at all', 'Very nice! But descending to the crater is very dangerous' and 'Truly beautiful, but know what to expect!' One reviewer even described his descent into the Ijen Crater and the limited oxygen in the toxic sulphur air. The thought of climbing down a steep volcanic crater in the dark with limited oxygen and a gas mask covering my face crippled me with fear.

We began weighing up whether or not we should use the guide we had been recommended. The mixed online reviews had us even more confused and not knowing just how difficult the climb would be was terrifying. But, after much deliberation, we decided not to hire the guide, as he was also bringing a large group of Italian tourists, and the last thing I wanted was to be under pressure to keep up with a brisk group of people on a steep uphill climb in the early hours of the morning.

With that decided, we set our alarms and turned out the lights, not that it did much to darken the room — after all, it was still only 6:30 p.m. The noise of trucks and farmers going about their day at the neighboring Javan coffee factory echoed around the room. However, it wasn't the commotion outside or the hot, bright room keeping me awake — it was this new sense of fear.

We woke at midnight and it was time to move. We hoisted our heavy backpacks onto our backs and shuffled out to meet our driver. He looked as exhausted as we were but still greeted us with a warm smile and two Styrofoam breakfast boxes. We spread the jam around the sliced bread in a zombie-like motion; we had little interest in eating but knew it was a necessity.

After a short drive, we arrived at the carpark and quickly sourced our rented heavy coats and masks. While we were paying at the cash register, a can of Guinness caught my eye. I chuckled to myself and thought that even though I was over 12,000 kilometres from Ireland and about to climb a 2799-metre volcano, I was never too far from home.

We laughed and joked with our driver as he wished us the best of luck and said he'd be waiting asleep in the carpark. With the cold air making its way to our bones, we made a last-minute purchase and donned some woolly gloves as we took off into the night. The black path, nearly vertical, danced under the light of our head torches. Each step felt like a calf muscle stretch but on we went, one foot in front of the other.

After what felt like our fifteenth break, I began to question if I could really complete the trek. I was exhausted from the previous two days and frustrated with myself for thinking we could fit three major hikes into three days. I wasn't sure what I feared more, continuing on or the thought of being left behind the procession of hikers in the cold air and dark night. As we climbed, the air grew thinner, and it became harder to breathe. I was out of breath but realized I'd soon have to breathe through the mask anyway.

When we finally reached the top of the volcano, we fixed our masks over our faces and began to descend into the crater. Each footstep was strategically placed, and the procession of hikers had quickly turned into a slow and steady string of head torches hypnotically decorating the crater's edge.

I took advantage of the slower pace by taking a minute to enjoy my surroundings. It felt out of this world, moon-like even. I was breathless in every sense of the word.

Abrupt yelling then broke through my trance: 'Move back, move back — let the miner through.' We had read about the local miners in multiple online reviews; how they carry a load of sulphur up to 90 kilograms on their shoulders. Tommy had warned me that it might be tough to see. I scrambled out of the way and looked back to make sure others had done so, too.

Out of the darkness appeared a man, short in stature and covered in dust with his head hung low beneath the weight. He made his way up from the crater, passing the tourists one by one, carrying two reed baskets full of bright yellow sulphur — what they call 'devil's gold'. As he navigated past me, my heart broke at the thought of his exertion and suffering. My eyes followed him up the crater, and suddenly the procession began to move again. I looked back, but he had faded into the darkness, leaving as abruptly as he had arrived. We carried on, passing several other sulphur miners going about their night's work, each one making my heart heavier.

When we reached the crater's floor, we were captivated by Ijen's famous blue flames. But it wasn't just the brilliance of the blue flames that caught my eye; I was fixated on a figure throwing a metal pole violently at the flames in an attempt to mine the solidified sulphur slabs. I moved closer and as I did, the figure ran towards me and buckled over, coughing ferociously. When he looked up, his eyes met mine, and he removed the wet rag that was tied tight around his mouth and nose, revealing a fatigued young face.

I stared at him, looking alien-like in my mask, watching this human being working in completely inhumane conditions. I had feared the steep uphill hike; I had feared the dark and cold night; I had feared not being able to breathe, but those fears seemed trivial compared to the young man playing with blue fire.

The Stranger

KELTOUM KOUAOUCI

I - PARANOIA

Standing amid the thick crowd at La place Maurice-Audin,
I flinched under the blazing glare of Monsieur Meursault
that seemed to pierce like a cannonball through the back of
my bare head, urging me to look up.

As I spun my head around in search of the nonchalant
silhouette that had abruptly vanished, a slap of eastern
wind awakened my once-asleep logic, as well as my
agony, and I realized three fundamental truths at the exact
same time: one, that my bare head was not really bare
because I could feel the mandated veil cool with sweat
around my head; two, that Monsieur Meursault was the
protagonist of the novel *The Stranger* by Albert Camus,
which I had read back in the summer, and there was no
way he'd be watching me now; and three, I had let my
mind go astray again, and now I was lost.

The fast cars and traffic lights of Algiers were overwhelming, and by the time I got to the other side of the road, my heart was flopping down into my belly, making me question whether I had been correct in my decision to study here.

A plain marble sign that read *'Lycée International Alexandre-Dumas'* caught my eye, and I smiled faintly as a large gate opened and a maddening crowd of teenagers mumbling loudly in French pushed me to the side. Not understanding a word, I stood limp against the sign with a biting rush behind my eyelids reminding me of my own hollowness.

I remembered my sister's instructions to head straight, away from my university's gate once my classes ended and to not stop until I was in a bus station. And if I got lost? 'Just ask someone.'

As I approached a girl my age outside the university gate, I tried to gather enough courage to ask her about the bus, but the words ended up piled into a lump in my throat, declaring yet another failed attempt to vocalize my thoughts. Another girl came my way, and this time I prepared in my head what to say in a fake central accent. The girl told me that the school buses stopped working at 5:00 p.m. it was now 5:45 p.m. and I started to panic.

I stood on the grounds that had been roamed by Monsieur Meursault, 'The Stranger' himself, and I couldn't help but feel like a stranger myself. I knew the grounds reeked, but I didn't smell anything. I just wanted my home.

Girls become notorious once they leave home and attend a boarding school, people had told me. People start calling them names, bad names. I'd been here only one night, but I had already had several encounters with them. They were nice, cooked us dinner, prayed (me and my sister didn't), and then started telling stories about men — dirty stories. I allowed myself to laugh along, for what they did any girl here would do.

A bus eventually arrived, and I took it. I headed to the driver to hand him the fee, but the passengers laughed at my foolish gesture. An old lady assured me that another collector would come to get the money. I was supposed to get off at the bus station of Ben Aknoun, but I didn't know where that was nor what it looked like, so I asked a woman wearing giant glasses if she was going there. She nodded, and I made a mental note to follow her. But I lost sight of her and, to stop the feeling of nausea, I got off the next time the bus stopped.

I was in a place that didn't look quite like a station. I asked yet another woman and she told me that the station I needed was still far away. Looking at my face, she shook her head and asked me where I was headed, and although I knew she might have already guessed from my accent, I still felt ashamed and told her a half truth: 'Deli Ibrahim'. She nodded her head and told me not to panic. She waited with me for another bus and instructed the collector to make sure I arrived safely at the station.

Once in Deli Ibrahim, I was shaken as my surroundings came to light; pretty girls tossing their silky hair from side to side, speaking fluent French and smoking rolled cigarettes, the pretense of me reading a book on my lap ... A guy nudged my arm and I was brought back to reality. He asked if I was after a fun, late car ride. I ran all the way to the girls' dormitory and up the building's stairs until I was with my sister and our roommate. They started asking about my first day at university when my cheap phone vibrated and Papa's first words were, *'Oui, ça va, ma puce?'* ('How are you, my darling?') I hung up and started crying.

II - FRIENDSHIPS AND ADVENTURES

He slipped his soft hand through mine, locking our fingers together and guiding me through streets that once gave me panic. On the other side of the road, he casually threw his arm around my shoulders, and I lifted my gaze to his, struck that I'd never held hands with a boy nor been this close to one. I beamed at him and declared that lunch was on me. 'Oh, baby girl,' he countered, 'don't let big boys take advantage of you!'

It's nice to have a friend, I thought.

Ween l-Hmam, or the Birds' Place, had become the best place for my friends and I to hang out. It was where we ate lunch, laughed at boyfriends, and teased each other about our clothes and our eccentric obsessions. And I couldn't shake the feeling that a few months ago I couldn't pass this very street without feeling panic because a bunch of teenagers had started talking in French.

Now I roamed all of Algiers with my best friend. She showed me tricks about how to flirt with boys. We mounted the ancient stairs leading up to Notre-Dame d'Afrique, shared a meal and she stood up for us when a guy with red, bloodshot eyes told us that we lacked manners because we had jumped the fence, instead of taking the gate like ladies. She turned heads as we walked, and I felt proud.

We rode the subway, and she joked about me not knowing how to use it, being a small-town girl. I fired back that we came from nearly the same district. We laughed aloud and lost sight of the time as we moved through thrift stores.

Sneaking into the dormitory, crying in the room, doing make-up, venturing the scary halls for evidence and trying to solve the case of the girl who was found dead in her room, telling stories and blasting our brains to the radio, I realized I'd never had a real friend before.

Catching free buses, counting our money on the bare streets for the Museum of Fine Arts, hacking online sites for free movies, marching with our creative signs, dancing in circles singing old, local football rhymes, stopping to pet every cat we saw, watching all Algiers from the Martyrs' Memorial, I realized I'd never lived before, I'd never had a family of pals.

III - AGAIN, BUT BETTER
OCTOBER, 2019

'1, 2, 3, 4, 5,' I counted in my head whenever someone talked to me. It usually took me up to 30 for them to bring up the magical question, 'You have an accent! You're not from here, are you?'

A year later, and a year wiser, I'd loved and I'd lost, but I was still only eighteen and on fire. I looked back on the days when I first came to the city and smiled at the baby

I was. 'You're not awkward, you're just innocent,' a friend once told me.

Feeling out of place has its perks, for it doesn't only make you treasure what, in the snap of a finger, has become out of reach, but it also, during the darkest of your nights, makes you stumble on a secret power — the power of letting go, the power of stepping upon your fears and living, despite it all.

Believing in Nothing

JADE DE LA ROSA

I was twelve years old when I stopped believing in God and started believing in my death. The thrilling drop of the plane was turbulence, no longer a fun game, and the rings of the cabin weren't playful sounds but signs that I had survived take-off — for now.

I wasn't always like this, but within a matter of days, flying became a life-risking act.

For several years, flying meant nightmares of hijacked planes and crashes so fiery that I awoke in a sweat. On the plane, my hands felt as though they could melt the armrest. At take-off I closed my eyes and played music loud enough to drown out the thrust of the engines, and during turbulent air I would grip the hand of my Mom, or whoever happened to be doomed to a flight with me that day.

Once, on a flight to Hawaii, our plane began its slow and

uneventful descent into Kona. We were landing late, and the plane carved its way through the black sky, lowering so close to the ground that we could see waves lapping the shore. Suddenly the engines roared, my heart exploded and panic rushed up through my body faster than our plane took off — an aborted landing. Did those exist?

In the seat next to me, my brother imitated the crash that hadn't happened.

'Boom!' he said, his body seizing. He cradled his hands over his head and swung himself forward in the seat. 'We're crashing, we're crashing!'

'Stop,' I whispered. I was afraid that if I spoke louder, I might cause the plane to actually crash.

'Boom!' he said again. His cheeks were red.

The plane hit turbulence, the cabin rocking as though falling over big waves. I was seasick in the sky.

'Please, stop,' I begged, but fear was too fun for a younger brother. Suddenly my clenched hand, clammy with sweat, swung upwards and punched him in the face.

He looked at me, blinking. The plane stilled.

'I'm so sorry,' I said and meant it, but he glared at me from beneath his swollen black eye for the rest of the trip.

This was a problem. My parents needed me to fly. There would be family trips, visits to Tanzania and Fiji and the Netherlands. There was college. There was the rest of my life ahead of me.

'The rest of my land-locked life,' I corrected.

'That's no fun,' my Mom said. 'Think of everything you'll miss out on.'

'I'll take a boat. Or a bus.'

She said nothing.

In college, my Mom drove me down to Seattle, Washington, every week from our home outside of Vancouver, British Columbia, to see a hypnotist. If it worked for quitting smoking, losing weight, insomnia, addiction and depression, it would work for a fear of flying — or so we were told.

'Close your eyes,' the hypnotist said as I settled into a chair. She draped a blanket around me. Her voice was soothing, each syllable drawn out as though we had infinite time here in the stuffy room together.

'You're on the plane,' she whispered, 'and so excited to go on this trip.'

'Okay,' I said. 'I can do this.'

I could play make-believe.

I imagined myself booking plane tickets, heading through the airport with a smile spread wide across my face. In this dream, there is no airport security because nothing bad can happen. I board the plane; the seats are wide, the other passengers are friendly, and we sail into the sky so quickly that I don't even realize we've already taken off.

She sent me home with a CD to play on my laptop. I was instructed to listen to these recordings twice a day, and more leading up to a flight. For several months I kept my promise, letting her words lull me to sleep each night and occasionally between classes, but when I got on a plane for another family trip back to Hawaii, my anxiety spiked.

'And you're listening to these every day?' my Mom asked as I gripped her hand. We were somewhere above the blue Pacific. I stared out the window, trying to focus my attention on each wave. Could you see whales from the sky?

'Yes,' I said, but my voice was so small I don't think she heard me.

Sometime between getting home from a trip to Hawaii and finishing college, I stopped listening to those audio tapes. I didn't miss them, and I had never not gotten on a plane. My fears were real, I reasoned, but not crippling.

Years later I chose to study a graduate program in Vermont, 3000 miles away from where I was now living with my husband in San Diego, California. It was a low-residency program, but I was required to attend ten-day-long residencies twice a year. Months away from my starting date, the flight seemed doable, maybe even enjoyable. I'd take the red-eye to maximize time at home and save on expenses. But as the departure date approached, my nightmares increased. I was on a plane suspended in the sky until the world dropped away and I was falling; I was on a flight with so much turbulence that attendants tumbled across the aisle. The day before, I had packed my bag with so much trepidation that I felt nauseous. I said goodbye to my husband at the airport, tears gathering in the corners of my eyes — not because of the days we'd be apart, but because of the minutes until my flight took off.

I got through check-in, security, and to my gate before I turned around and went home. My bag was delivered to me a day later. It had travelled to Vermont and back, unopened, without me.

While my classmates were listening to lectures and taking part in workshops on the other side of the country, I Googled fear of flying classes. I needed help. One website looked reputable; the owner of the company was a former pilot himself, but the class was offered in Phoenix, Arizona. That meant I would need to fly to Phoenix to take a class that would involve a short return flight, and then fly home again. No, thank you!

My husband and I then moved back to the rain shadows of the Pacific Northwest and away from my family in San Diego. I dearly missed my Mom. For days a tab on my computer stayed open: flights from Seattle to San Diego. I debated making the purchase, not for lack of funds but because it would sentence me to another flight, and worse, a flight of my own choosing. As Mother's Day approached, in a maddening rush, I booked a ticket there and back, by myself.

My husband drove me to the airport. We went around and around, looking for parking so that he could walk me in. Though he grew frustrated looking for an empty spot, I hoped we'd never find one. My throat closed in tight and my jaw ached when we finally pulled into a parking space.

'I can't do this,' I said.

'Yes, you can,' he said.

'What happens if I don't go?' I wiped hot tears away.

'Nothing.'

I didn't have to ask what would happen if I did go. I hugged my husband goodbye, then rolled my bag toward the terminal.

For all the times my Mom had held my hand, not holding hers on Mother's Day would mean the absence of a memory that might have been.

Not going would mean nothing had happened. And for that, I went.

Where Are You From? Where Are You Going?

JOE AULTMAN-MOORE

We're afraid of the wrong people.

Our first time out of the country, my brother Ben and I spent months hitchhiking around Ireland. We travelled in dozens of cars meeting a cross-section of Ireland in its drivers: a bed-and-breakfast owner, a civil servant, a university student. Men and women, of all ages and professions. People's lives flashed by as we jumped cars like stepping stones across a river.

One sour young man wanted to know if we were scared of being robbed by Gypsies. I said I didn't think we'd come across any. He snorted in disbelief, 'Jaysus, lads — the Gypsies, the Travellers, feckin' Tinkers! Don't trust 'em. They'll rob you blind or worse.'

'But who are they? How do we know?'

He spat out the window. 'You'll know. They go around in feckin' horse-drawn carts, live in these big camps around the edges of towns. Something different-looking about 'em too. Just don't trust 'em.'

Most drivers were genial and chatty, and some invited us to dinner or to stay in their houses with their families. Others were suspicious. But only one stood out as a truly *bad* ride.

* * *

We were on the side of the N24 to Kilkenny, where our previous ride had dropped us off. It was a bad spot — too fast and too little shoulder. It's illegal to hitchhike on a motorway in Ireland, so we had our thumbs out nervously, expecting to be stopped by the *Gardaí* (the Guards) any minute. Raining and cold, the road was long, wide and wet as a river. Cars rocketed by.

We stood there aching when a tiny white car passed us, pulled off the road, and then, to our surprise, went in reverse on the shoulder and stopped beside us. I jumped in shotgun (in Ireland, that's on the left), crunching paper cups and bags, and Ben got in the back. We introduced ourselves to the driver.

'Andy,' he said through a cigarette and peeled the car back onto the motorway. He looked like a stray dog crouched over the wheel. Middle-aged, an outdoors-worn face, with strong hands with dirty fingernails. He asked the standard questions of where we were from and where we were going. I was settling into the answers when he interrupted, 'Do you drink beer?'

'Sorry?'

'Beer.' He didn't wait for my answer but reached down and handed me a can of Tudor Beer, tossed one back to Ben and then cracked one open for himself. 'To new friends,' he toasted.

Sometimes the mind runs through excuses, justifications for why you don't need to get out of the car, why you don't need to stand on the side of the road again. *Ah, one beer, what's one beer?* I've driven with one beer before.

'So, Andy, where are you from?' I asked.

'Just outside Kilkenny. Got me a little dairy farm. Lovely town, Kilkenny. You lads would love it there. Don't bother with Dublin, nothing but feckin' gobshites there.'

'Do you have any family there? Married?'

'Not married, no …' Andy trailed off, then he said with a yellow toothy grin, 'The girl I'm with now, when we first moved to Kilkenny, we pulled this trick in some of the pubs.' As he talked, he flicked his cigarette and reached into the glove compartment for a pouch of tobacco and rolling papers. He put his knees on the wheel and rolled another cigarette on his lap. 'Anyway, she was getting chatted up by some rich-looking fecker. I pretend that I'm her brother. So now this ugly feck's buying both of us pints.' Andy glanced between his lap and the road.

'Would you like me to roll that for you?' I asked.

'No, no, no. It's no trouble. So, he's buying us pints and goes to take a piss. Me and me girl go out front for a fag. She thinks it's all a grand joke and kisses me. So, we're shifting and the rich fecker walk out and sees us. I've even got the man's beer in my hand, right. The look on his face! He says, "with her brother!"'

We laughed uproariously and Andy reached for another beer. Two beers, so what, you're not drunk after two beers.

∗ ∗ ∗

The car screeched onto the shoulder and Andy got out, 'I've got to take a piss.' He slammed the door shut.

'This guy's scaring the shit out of me,' Ben said.

'Look, it's not the safest ride we've taken, but he's only had a beer and a half. He's not driving too crazy, and we're making good time to Kilkenny.'

'No, listen, there's an empty six-pack back here ...'

The car door opened and Andy sloped in. 'Ahhh, we'll get you there, lads!' He grinned, under at least eight beers of good cheer. Another cigarette and the car screeched back onto the road, and the speedometer went up like a pressure cooker into the triple digits.

'Feck, I know a good guy in Kilkenny, he'll put you up for the night. Good, solid guy. Feckin' alcoholic, but solid.'

The car sped down the narrow side roads, barely wider than the side mirrors. Andy began to sing low and gravelly,

'Waaay out upon the Swanee River, far far away ...' A T-intersection appeared ahead and it was coming towards us much too fast. I looked over and Andy was trying to roll another cigarette on his thigh, one hand on the wheel.

'Andy!' I shouted. He looked up and screeched on the brakes; we skid out into the intersection.

'Feckin' hell, where did that shite come from?'

Cascades of adrenaline ran like cold water down my back.

'Waaay out upon the Swanee River ...' Andy sang through a cigarette. I was plastered to my chair, soaked in ice water. No peep from the backseat as Ben was as petrified as I. A sign whipped by: Kilkenny 20 kilometres. God, we'll be mashed into oblivion long before that!

A new fear: what if Andy refused to let us out? I wanted to be anywhere: a burning building, the middle of the ocean, a desert island — anywhere but the inside of that car. 'Hey, Andy, these are some great camping spots we're passing up, how about just dropping us off here?'

'Naw, I'll bring you to this guy, he's solid as feck, you'll see.'

'No, really, Andy, that's a great spot right there. Just right THERE!'

'Eh, if you're sure.' The car veered to the side and screeched to a halt and we stumbled out into the drizzle like escaping prisoners. Andy sped off and I kissed the sweet Irish earth. I'm alive!

Ben and I sat on the shoulder, letting the adrenaline diffuse. Another car stopped for us before we even stuck out our thumbs. To our relief, it was an old gentleman who preached to us about the evils of alcohol.

✳ ✳ ✳

Kilkenny. Strange night in a strange town with no plans, no acquaintances and not enough money for a hotel. So, we walked back out of Kilkenny. Exhausted and heavy, we just wanted to stop and rest; we just needed a spot of flat ground wide enough to pitch a tent on. But the rows of houses went on and on, every inch of land spoken for. We didn't belong.

Out at the edge of town, there was a break in the fence of a wheat field. We could see a dirt path ahead and decided to follow it, our vision only as wide as the little circles of light from our headlamps.

The silhouette of a large building appeared under a sliver of moonlight. We'll just go up and ask if we can stay; if they refuse, we'll move on, no harm done. Wheat rustled and swished against our clothes, acres and acres of wheat. Something was odd though; there were no warm lights and there was no car. The building was huge though — a farmhouse? The light from our headlamps seemed to spray some detail onto the scene — countless windows, every single one with rotten boards nailed across it. This place, though, had not been accounted for nor claimed. This was the edge, where travellers belong.

'Hellooo?' I called into the dark, my voice sounding both

tiny and large. Wind. We camped around back. All was quiet, no one was there.

Or so we thought.

✳ ✳ ✳

In the morning I stepped out for a look around and realized there were people on the other side of the house. I ran back to the tent and shook Ben awake. We had to get out of here. We quickly stripped down the tent, threw everything in our packs and started speed-walking out the back, grateful for the tall wheat. We could see five figures at the house, maybe more. And horses. They were distracted, not expecting two strangers running through their backyard.

'They're Gypsies,' Ben whispered and, of course, it made sense. I felt a strange pang of fear and suspicion, the virus passed to us days ago by the sour young man.

As we approached the fence thinking at any second the Gypsies will turn and see us, down the road came a horse-drawn cart. Wearing old, patched-up clothes and with unruly boy-hair, two pairs of brothers sat across from each other in the cart on an otherwise empty road in Ireland.

The older one stopped and asked us questions, blunt but not unfriendly, with a strange accent not exactly Irish, *'Whir ye from? Whir ye gooin?'*

He was no more than fifteen but had fiery eyes and the stern hawk-face of an older man. I saw the mirror of who I might have been under different circumstances. I saw that we are afraid of those who are most nearly like ourselves and that the most dangerous people in the world are those that are a danger to themselves.

The boy flicked the reins, the horse trundled on and he hummed low a song that I barely made out, 'Waaay out upon the Swanee River, far far away ...'

Fearless Footsteps on Mount St Helens

CAROL ROSE CUPPY

I took a step and slid backwards. The gray ash shifted to fill in the print of my boot as if I had never even stepped there. The volcano could erase me just as quickly — the softest of all tremors beneath my boots reminded me of that. I swallowed the ripple of fear that told me the volcano could erupt at any moment and continued my climb up Mount St Helens' steep slope.

The summit was close. After three gruelling miles trekking through thick forest and a maze of massive boulders, the grey, jagged line of the rim set itself firmly against the crisp, blue sky. White glaciers streaked down the volcano's cone to my left as white dots shuffled over the snowy surface in the distance — a family of white mountain goats cooling off in the heat of the day. Just 20 feet to my right was a massive ravine. One slip; that's all it would take for search and rescue to find me at the bottom.

My hiking partners and I had set out early that morning to make an attempt on Mount St Helens' summit. The trailhead starts on the south side of the mountain, nestled in a clump of forest so thick a cougar could be stalking you and you'd never notice. From the Climber's Bivouac Trailhead, the volcano looks like any other mountain — there's no trace of the devastation from the 1980 eruption. The north side of Mount St Helens, however, is a completely different story.

We had trekked through the 1980 blast zone only a couple days before. The entire north face of Mount St Helens now lies completely open, revealing a growing lava dome perched in the middle of a mile-wide crater. On May 18, 1980, a 5.1 magnitude earthquake triggered a landslide on the volcano's northern slopes. The sudden release in pressure allowed magma that had been building inside the volcano to explode like a shaken soda can. All of that erupted material — ash, pyroclastic flows, lava bombs, even intact chunks of the mountain called hummocks — buried the landscape. Trees were ripped from their stumps and still lay, decades later, pointing south to north, showcasing the direction of the blast. The eruption annihilated the forest and nearly everything in it for up to 20 miles, killing 57 people in its wake.

Ash up to my calves, I took another step up towards the summit. I was acutely aware of how much energy was pulsing through the volcano beneath my feet. While I was confident that I was prepared for this climb, the truth was that volcanoes are notoriously unpredictable. An eruption could happen anywhere, anytime. A sudden burst of ash could suffocate me, falling rocks might crush me, or a pyroclastic flow could vaporize me. If the mountain so much as shuddered, the resulting landslide could bury me right there.

And, nevermind that 24 hours ago I'd had a seizure.

My body is notorious for inventing creative ways to rebel. That, in itself, causes more fear when travelling than anything I've ever done, including strolling up an active volcano. I've had Crohn's disease for a decade now, and the pain, exhaustion, and constant need for a bathroom keeps me chained to civilization. Daring to hike away from a functioning toilet? That's living dangerously.

I'd had a plan in place for today's hike, but the plan was disturbed when my body threw a grand mal seizure on me — right in the middle of a mountain sports store. My body shook violently for five minutes, giving me the workout of the century. I spent the entire day before our summit attempt at a Portland hospital when I should have been stuffing my backpack and relaxing. The emergency doctor insisted that I ditch the hike. 'Don't go up that mountain tomorrow. You need to rest. Hike it another day.'

Those words struck more fear in me than anything. It was the fear of missing out on a hike I'd craved since childhood. It took the four of us exactly five minutes to decide that we were going to show up at the trailhead that Tuesday morning and hike as far as we could. And at this point, it was looking like the summit was within our grasp.

But the seizure had taken its toll on my body. My muscles were aching and cramping, and I was exhausted. It was worse than having the flu. More challenging still, the mountain kept tipping and spinning under my boots. Vertigo was suddenly a real thing; so was the bottom of the chasm next to me. One wrong step was all it would take for my volcano-climbing career to be over.

I paused and leaned against my hiking poles. For a moment I thought, 'Why am I even out here?'

Because I love volcanoes. They have fascinated me since the first moment I spotted a lava flow in my third-grade science book. A passion for their fiery might is what brings me back time and time again to explore their slopes and to get to know their different personalities.

So, you gonna climb me, or what? I could practically hear Mount St Helens' challenge. Straightening my shoulders and digging my poles in, I took another step, and another, right up the back of the volcano.

The mile-wide crater spread in front of me as I reached the summit, the side slopes spread wide like an eagle's wings. The scale of the ever-growing lava dome in the heart of the crater was intimidating. If I were to stand on it, I'd be no more than a speck against its layers of black lava. The reek of sulphur, like rotten eggs, made my nose burn and my eyes sting. Rocks tumbled down the crater's slopes with a sound like shaken dice. I could clearly see the contours of the 1980 blast zone where we had hiked just a few days before. Mount Rainier, Mount Adams and Mount Hood — each mighty volcanoes themselves — surrounded Mount St Helens to the north, east, and south like sentinels.

This moment was worth every scrape and scratch I had endured on the climb. It was worth every dizzying, heart-stopping moment when I had slipped on the ash. Finding myself off the beaten path and staring into the heart of the most active volcano in North America meant more to me now because of the fear I'd faced and conquered.

But reaching the summit only marked the halfway point of our journey. It had taken us twice as long to reach Mount St Helens' peak than we had planned. Now the four of us had to get down the volcano's slopes, and the sun was slipping fast toward the western horizon.

Puffs of ash rose around our heels as we dashed through the ash field. The vibrant oranges and pinks of the sunset washed over the hills as the sun dipped below the horizon. At the upper edge of the boulder field, next to a seismic monitor, we paused to catch our breath. Chunks of lava larger than a Jeep were strewn everywhere. We were going to have to navigate the maze of lava in the dark.

Our headlamps were the only light for miles around. The Milky Way filled the black sky with a spray of stars and disappeared into the glow that was Portland. I clutched my hiking poles in one hand and clung to the boulders with the other as we descended. Spiders raced over the toes of my boots and the backs of my gloves. I bit back a shriek, but the fear of losing my grip on the volcano was far stronger than my fear of spiders.

It took us several hours to navigate the boulder field, and the forest was a welcome sight simply because there was a trail there. However, the blackness beneath the trees was suffocating. Who knew what lurked behind the ferns and bushes? Cries of 'Shoo, kitty!' and 'Here, bear!' echoed through the forest ahead of me as my partners in crime blazed the trail, on the lookout for bears and cougars. We passed a pair of hikers who were just beginning their ascent, hoping to reach the ash field by sunrise.

We burst from the forest into the Climber's Bivouac Trailhead at 2:00 a.m. sharp, thinking of Sir Edmund Hillary's words: 'It is not the mountain we conquer but ourselves.' Just the day before, my body had conquered me. Today, it had been my turn. We had summited the volcano, unearthing the courage that lay beneath the dried lava on the slopes of Mount St Helens and buried our fear in its place.

The Ocean Needed a Vacation

MONICA ZAVALA-PERETTO

'Can I smoke in here?' she asked as they stared at the ocean view in front of them.

'Facing the West Wind like this, air doesn´t linger here very long.'

'There is a bug in your water.'

'There is a van backseat in the palmas.'

'There is water and sand in the oven. Maybe it´s Carlos, Fondo …'

'There is sand in the oven?'

***

Warning: Don't go to Mexico, says the US State Department's travel website. The risks are car-jacking, drug smuggling, kidnapping, natural disasters. Specifically, they say for the state of Oaxaca: *'Oaxaca, Huatulco, and Puerto Escondido are major cities/travel destinations in Oaxaca — No advisory is in effect.'* The beach resort of Zipolite didn't make the cut.

So, are we safe here? This is what I asked during my third year of immersing myself in the peace and love of Playa Zipolite. As a Mexican–American or an American–Mexican, I moved to Mexico to get to know my roots. My master's degree landed me a job at *Universidad del Mar*, the local university, as an English teacher. Though Oaxaca is nowhere near my family in Guanajuato, it was much more appealing than the other offers I got in the more inland states closer to them. Since I had arrived, family and friends in both countries were always asking questions about safety and fear. Are you near the drug cartel? Is there violence? Can you drink the water? Have you been robbed? Are there tsunamis?

Locals say people don't end up here by accident. They're called to this place known as 'Lost in Time', the 'Laid-back Beach', or 'Hippie Heaven of Mexico'. They emphasize that Zipolite, translated from the local Zapotec dialect, means 'Beach of the Dead' and will tell you about the red riptide flags the lifeguards use to warn the locals and tourists of unsafe swimming. The world didn't end in 2012 as suggested by the Mayans, but during the beginning of the rainy season in early May 2015, I had my first taste of an uncontrollable fear, exaggerated by the outside world, when we were hit by a phenomenon called *mar de fondo* — the swelling of the ocean generated by storms at sea and high winds.

Someone said the waves got so high they far surpassed Roca Blanca Avenue, which sits about 100 metres from the beach and over 75 feet above sea level.

✳ ✳ ✳

One-hundred-and-fifty metres from the shore, a father stood atop a table holding his one-year-old daughter as they watched the logs that supported the *palapa* roof receive a quick water-punch to the knees and fall down in seconds. The roof he had built for her was being washed away by the force of the ocean waves. They watched plastic kitchen items, and the tables and benches he had built continue on with the wave into their new home at sea. They watched his van, containing his music equipment, sink into the sand and rapidly fill with water, gradually inching away from them, as if some giant transformer had lifted it up and moved it. The rush of the water forced the backseat through the open door and the van crashed into the wall next to them. As he embraced his daughter tightly against his chest, they watched this.

He had been in the process of cooking his daughter's next meal.

✳ ✳ ✳

If you ask the hippies, they will tell you that the ocean needed a vacation. There was too much negativity and movement was necessary.

If you ask the professors, they will tell you it's stupid to live on a shore nicknamed 'Beach of the Dead'. They know this can happen.

If you ask the expats, they will tell you a sad story about a third-world country that doesn't have firefighters nor a well-developed, government-organized natural disaster team. They don't have *mar de fondo* drills in *primaria* (primary school).

✳ ✳ ✳

A short distance down the beach from where that first wave hit, a mother rushed to grab her baby from across the one-room concrete house they lived in. The wave knocked over a pile of clothes and the stacked dishes. It stole a pitcher, silverware, pots and pans, many clothes and baby toys, and broke the shelf of shot glasses right above the window. They could have been trapped and drowned instantly if it hadn't been for the back door where the water was able to push through. After the first wave subsided, the adrenaline rush made the mother reflect on the ability, power, and the unexpectedness of the ocean. She never expected the second wave to hit or what the weeks to come would bring.

Her baby had just fallen asleep. She was going to take a shower.

* * *

If you ask the mayor, he will tell you that he is working to bring the families some food and a care package of small necessities. They will come a few weeks too late after the majority of those affected have already resettled without those care packages.

If you ask the locals that live on the hill, they will tell you *Gracias a Dios* ('Thank God') the waves didn't make it up that far. They feel bad for the shoreline folks, and believe their life is just as hard-working to ensure water, gas, electricity and food can arrive on a daily basis as well. They will not tell you but guide you into understanding that 'life is more difficult when it's always uphill.'

If you ask the children, they will run around the next day, closer than they should be to the sea, away from every wave that comes up yelling *'fondo'* and laughing as the waves break at their feet.

* * *

After the second wave hit and subsided, some families frantically tried to grab the rest of their lost items from various directions on the beach and some stood staring around, with their arms on necks pinching the stress right out of them. When the emergency response team finally arrived in their big trucks, they carried loaded assault rifles, ready for the man versus the ocean fight. They didn't help the families collect, organize and straighten up. Rather, in their neatly pressed shirts with a yellow safety strip, they wrote down names and took many pictures. They double-checked the spelling of names. There was no community dinner being prepared for the affected families that night, but their shirts tucked in tightly into their pants and sealed with that official belt made the town feel protected.

Restaurants raised an order of tacos from 30 to 60 pesos.

* * *

If you ask some of the locals, they will tell you those blithering idiots should have been more prepared.

If you ask the volunteer lifeguards, they will tell you they are always prepared to jump in and help when a crisis hits because they know it's their duty. With yet another natural tragedy, they will tell you they are thankful the response team 'did all they could in the matter tending to the shore community as quickly as possible.' They will tell you their story for their few minutes of fame.

* * *

After the *mar de fondo*, families continued to walk the beach looking for their lost possessions, gazing at other people's damaged homes. The heavy wooden stairs of Cabañas La Habana ended up in the neighbour's yard. The stove of restaurant Sal y Pimiento was washed out to sea. Bang Bangs Bar lost its bar, and what was left was stolen by thieves — liquor bottles that hadn't shattered, and a few floating cans of beer. The 4-foot bar of Bang Bangs ended up on the beach at Colibri, and Café Maya was completely destroyed. That pink plastic *jarra* (pitcher) made it all the way to the *laguna* (lagoon), along with other items, waiting for its owner to find it.

Those affected will use the new toothbrushes and eat tinned food from the mayor's care packages while discussing being in such a situation. They will receive, one month later, a 2-inch foam pad to replace their damaged mattresses that the government calls a bed. The tag will say: 'Support the system of civil protection. Prohibited to sell.'

* * *

If you ask anyone, they will say, at the end of the day, the ocean can and does whatever it wants. This is a part of life on the beach. Just last year, it stole Bang Bang's pool table. They replaced it with ping pong table because it's cheaper to restore when the ocean takes its pick. Help does come to the people, at the pace it needs to, creating movement away from the old. They have lived through this before. Water washes up time and time again, with and without real damage. It was just time ...

So, are we safe, Zipolite? Logically, it all depends on what

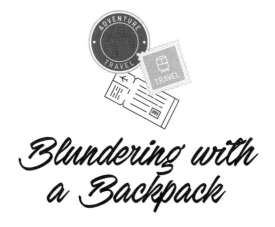

Blundering with a Backpack

LISA WATSON

I had been backpacking around Europe for four months and was so blasé about travelling that by the time I flew from London to Egypt I didn't even read a guidebook, let alone buy one for the 'just in case' scenario. I had come up with a vague plan that I would spend a week in Cairo seeing the sights, then make my way to a town somewhere down the coast to do a scuba-diving tour, which was the only thing I had booked.

For an experienced traveller this would have been no big deal, but I was far from it. Imagine a young woman growing up on an isolated sheep farm in New Zealand who sets off to see the world. Then think about how the flight to Egypt is only the second plane ride she has ever taken in her life, the first one being just a few months earlier when she flew to London. Sure, she knows how to shear a sheep and repair a tractor engine, but does she know anything about travelling? The answer is definitely 'no'. My trip was in the days long before smartphones and the Internet, so there was no way for me to inform myself easily about anything once I hit the ground in Egypt. To make things even more interesting, I had decided that it was too expensive to call my family or friends to tell them where I was going.

I was as on my own as it was possible to be.

Although I was arriving a week in advance, the tour group that was organizing the dive trip had offered to send a driver to meet me at the airport and take me to my hotel for an extra charge. I declined as I thought it would be a waste of money to pay for an escort. How hard could it be?

Misgivings about my travel ability started the minute I walked into the arrivals lounge in Cairo. A coil of fear unfurled in my stomach. I began to feel slightly nauseous. This wasn't like being in European airports at all! There were people everywhere, many yelling and gesticulating wildly, others sleeping along the walls, or sitting on the floor playing cards. All of them looked as though they had been there for days. The morass of bodies pushing and shoving each other that passed for an immigration queue snaked down the hall in a jumble of people, baggage, and crying children.

My chest tightened. I couldn't speak or understand any Arabic, it was 10 o'clock at night, and I was a young woman on her own. What had I done? I looked around wildly, thinking that maybe they might let me back on the plane. My eyes lit on a man in a suit holding a card up. To my enormous relief, the card had my name on it. The tour company must have sent someone after all! The fluttering dread that was spasming through me subsided. I skipped up to him, pointed at the name, and told him it was me.

He looked at his card, then at me and shook his head.

'I'm sorry,' he said, 'but the Lisa Watson I'm meeting is flying in from Frankfurt, not London.'

No matter how hard I tried to reason and plead with him, he remained adamant that I was the wrong Lisa Watson. Panic roared out of its hiding place, filling me to the brim. He must have seen that I was about to fall to pieces as he said, 'I'll help you to get through immigration, but then you are on your own.'

He grabbed my pack and shouldered his way through the crowds to the front of the mob with me following hard on his heels. He talked animatedly to one of the immigration officers. The officer took a quick look at me, shrugged his shoulders, stamped my passport and ushered me through. I was in! I waved goodbye to my benefactor and felt the knot in my stomach unravel.

Little did I know that my adventure to get to the hotel was still on the down-swing.

I walked out into the warm night and saw a line of cabs and ramshackle cars waiting on the road. Before parting ways, my savior had warned me, 'Do NOT, under any circumstances, take anything but the Black and White taxis, and do NOT pay more than 50 Egyptian pounds.'

I was accosted immediately by a Black and White taxi driver who offered to take me into Cairo for 100 Egyptian pounds. I dumped my heavy backpack on the ground in order to haggle better. We were in full arm-waving mode when I spotted a man running towards us. Before I could react, he grabbed my bag and started walking away quickly with it, while yelling over his shoulder, 'I'll take you for 30 pounds!'

The terrifying feeling of being in way over my head smashed into me again. I stared blindly at my retreating bag for a few seconds, frozen into inaction from fear, until the realization that my passport and everything I owned was disappearing. Adrenaline kicked in. I began to chase him. The first taxi driver sprinted past me. He managed to catch on to one strap of my backpack. A tug-of-war with the bag-snatcher started, each one trying the wrestle my luggage away from the other. I stood rooted to the spot, watching mutely. Thanks to a slick move that would have looked good in a wrestling competition, the bag-stealer deftly twisted the backpack out of the taxi driver's hands and took off running toward his car, motioning for me to follow him.

So, I did.

In calmer circumstances, I would not have made the ridiculous decision to let myself be pushed into a car with a stranger at midnight in a foreign country where I couldn't speak the language. At that moment, though, I was only thinking about my bag.

As we raced toward his vehicle, four men materialized from behind it. I felt as though I was in an action movie. One opened the passenger door, pushed me into the car and slammed the door behind me. The other three ran towards the Black and White taxi driver, blocking him from following us. The winner of my backpack threw himself across the bonnet, jumped in the car, and took off with a screech of tyres into the Egyptian traffic.

I drew a deep breath to calm my racing heart. The deep breath didn't work at all as the connection between my brain and eyes actually began to work again and registered the car's condition. For a start, it had no window on my side and no seatbelts. Only one of the headlights seemed to be working, and the dashboard had large holes in it. I put my hand on the car door and discovered that the handle to open it was broken off.

So, this was it. I was going to be killed for being unorganized. I would be taken out into the desert and dumped, all for my documents and some second-hand clothes. I mentally kicked myself for not calling my parents. I wished that I had put on socks without holes in them that day. It is very strange what passes through your mind when you think you are going to die. I squeezed my eyes shut in horror, then partially opened them to steal a glance at my would-be murderer. He seemed pretty cheerful for a killer. He sang along to the song playing on the transistor radio he had taped to the dashboard while weaving through the traffic and continuously tooting his horn. I took a harder look. Actually, he didn't seem terribly threatening at all and was definitely shorter than me. My sock issue became less pressing. I started to hatch a plan to overcome him in the fight I was sure we were going to have.

Then he started to talk.

He told me about his kids, all five of them, and about his

beloved city. We arrived in the center of Cairo. The murderer proudly drove me across a bridge spanning the Nile River so that I could see all the newly married couples taking photos of themselves in front of the dark water flowing below. I was shaking with relief. Why would he show me the sights before killing me? My terror dissolved in a rush. When I closed my eyes this time, it was to better feel the warm, jasmine-scented wind blowing on my face through the broken car window.

By the end of the drive, I was sorry to see him go. I waved goodbye to the retreating car, then turned and pushed open the swinging doors of my hotel.

I was finally in Egypt, after years of dreaming about it, and I felt more alive than ever before.

Losing my (Diving) Virginity

AMY MCMAHON

'Have you ever been diving before?' my instructor, Jon, asked me.

'Not in Thailand,' was my response, although a correct response would have been never. The only place I'd ever worn scuba gear was in a pool.

'You're in for a treat,' Jon responded, helping my cousin and I onto the boat. My cousin had completed her Open Water certification already. I had taken my initial lessons in Montana and opted to do my certification elsewhere since I wasn't especially interested in diving to look at trout (unlike a surprisingly large number of people in my class, including my father).

'Thailand has some of the clearest waters in the world,' Jon continued, flipping through some papers in his hand as we settled onto the boat. He paused. 'Oh. Which one of you is Amy?'

'Me,' I said, raising my hand like in a classroom.

'Ah. I see you're completing your certification. So, you' — he pointed at my cousin — 'can explore while we do a few tests. Sound good?'

We nodded and began the tricky process of inspecting and strapping on the gear.

Jon eyed me as he helped me adjust the regulator, noticing my shaking hands and clumsy fingers. 'Nervous?' he asked.

I managed to nod. 'Nervous' seemed like too tame a word to explain the panic that was threatening to choke me.

I had always wanted to dive. I'd been a lifelong swimmer and was confident in the water — and I had aced the pool section of my diving class. Diving in the open ocean was a new world, however, and one I was equally excited and terrified to explore.

Suddenly, the idea of diving seemed insane. I was going underwater, where humans can't breathe without the aid of a tank full of artificial air. Then there was the constant threat of the bends, which seemed to me primarily caused by user error. This did not bode well for me as I dropped my mask off the boat and Jon had to fish it out with a net before we were even in the water.

He wiped it down and handed it to me wryly. 'You might want to keep that on your face.'

'Right,' I said, trying to joke. 'I'm no Aquaman.'

Jon gave me a funny look but was distracted by my cousin throwing up over the side. She wasn't nervous — just very susceptible to motion sickness.

Jon looked between us. 'This should be fun.'

'Yes!' my cousin said, wiping off her mouth. Her spirits were not dampened by a little vomit.

The island of Ko Tao, a wild-looking spit of land rising like a giant, green turtle from the sea (Ko Tao means Turtle Island in Thai), moved slowly away as we motored through the water. From this distance, it looked truly idyllic, perched in the impossibly blue Gulf of Thailand.

The boat stopped when we were still well within view of our little tropical bungalow. I had a sudden, desperate wish that we were back in this haven — I'd happily overlook the ant infestation and the bucket-toilet to be on terra firma.

Jon helped me get into position and watched my form as I followed my cousin into the sea. I put my face in the water while we waited for Jon to enter (I had accidentally hit him in the face with my fin, dislodging his mask). I took a few testing breaths to calm myself. The air was drier and tasted a little strange but filled my lungs the same.

A burst of bubbles appeared near me ... Jon was there, motioning me to swim to the lead rope, which led down to the bottom and would serve as a marker for our entry and exit. Jon had advised me to use it as a guide, so I grabbed it like the literal lifeline it was but found I couldn't continue. My cousin was already descending, and Jon was floating nearby, waiting. My hands were immobile. Jon pointed down again, as if he thought I was confused about what to do.

I took a few deep breaths and looked up. The surface was so near, and we were hardly in deep water as I could see the bottom through that clear, tropical water, so I began my descent. This lasted all of two seconds, because I immediately ran into my next difficulty: equalizing my ears.

Equalizing is the process of blowing out the pressure in your ears, so your eardrums don't explode (forgive me for simplifying the science). I moved up and down the rope, trying to equalize at every step. When my ears gave that telltale 'pop!', I felt the knots in my stomach loosen.

Finally, I was able to relax and take in my surroundings. The bottom of the ocean didn't look like I had pictured it. Everything was so blue; even the brightly-colored coral had a blue tinge to their oranges and reds. When I reached Jon, he took my hand and brushed it above a nearby, hot-pink plant that was waving in the current. It retracted, making me jump, and bubbles of laughter floated out.

Christmas tree worms, Jon wrote on his little underwater tablet. I moved my hand over them a few more times before we moved on. It was the first time I had forgotten about my fears.

My cousin explored the strange rock formations, the coral beds, and the schools of fish flashing by while I completed my tasks. I was no natural. I continued to have ear pain, I kicked things I shouldn't have — like coral and faces (yes, Jon's face had yet another encounter with my fin) — and once, I popped to the surface in panic.

Yet, when I did a slow roll and glimpsed the sparkly

surface above me, or saw an immense ray move powerfully by, or spotted a foraging turtle, none of that mattered. It was a whole new world, and I was in love.

'So, how was it?' Jon asked when we surfaced.

I grinned at Jon, making an 'O' with my forefinger and thumb, the diving symbol for 'OK.' 'Amazing! I can't wait to do it again!' And I meant it.

Jon laughed as he began to climb the ladder. 'No true diver does that "OK" above the surface, Amy. Just dorks.'

A few hours later, basking in the glow of my first day of diving, I began to get a headache. My ears hurt, and a strange bruise began to bloom on my chest. As I tossed and turned that night, I remembered how I had popped up to the surface without a single safety stop.

I had the bends. I knew it. We were on a tiny island in the Gulf of Thailand and death was coming.

After a rough night, we woke up to a storm. I secretly hoped diving would be cancelled.

'No way!' Jon said at breakfast. 'These are the best kind of days to dive.'

'Amy thinks she has the bends,' my cousin told him. I reluctantly told Jon my symptoms and showed him the bruise under my collarbone.

He eyed it. 'That's probably from the boat. Remember when you ran into the pole?'

'Oh, yeah,' I said, feeling a trickle of relief.

'I don't think you have the bends,' Jon told me. 'Sorry, but you won't get out of diving that easy.'

Although I wasn't sure he was right — except maybe about the bruise — I got back on the boat.

I'd figured after that first fearful day that diving would get easier. However, I still felt my nerves rocket as we rode further away from our little bungalow towards a site called Shark Island.

'Do you think we'll see sharks?' my cousin asked, eagerly. I was too nervous to speak.

'It's not actually called Shark Island because of sharks,' Jon told us, 'but because the rock pinnacle is kind of shaped like one.'

We were there, all too soon. Today my hands were shaking so much Jon had to help me at every step. My cousin entered first so she could have a few minutes of privacy for her usual surface vomit, and Jon gestured for me to follow.

I stared at the water for a few minutes, unable to move. Jon put his hand on my shoulder, and I wondered if he was going to push me in.

'So, what's it gonna be, Bendy? In or out?'

I looked at him through my mask. He was equipped and ready to go, looking at ease, even in his bulky gear. I felt a bubble of hysteria threaten to pop in my throat.

'I can do this,' I croaked out. He gave me a gentle push, and I fell into the water, away from both the boat and my fear.

Up or Bust

HAYDEN MULLER

I was high above the town of Squamish in British Columbia, in a rock-climbing mecca; a dream that had finally become a reality. Life had plucked me from the dry, flat and scorching hot Central Queensland landscape and now had me perched precariously, fatigued, sweating and trembling from fear hundreds of metres above the valley floor. My scraped and sore fingers twisted and pulled on the slick rock edges, desperately trying to jam themselves into granite cracks and fissures, cranking on them in a desperate plea to keep my body attached to the rock face that I now clung to. I glanced down at Danny holding the rope, his eyes wide, and watched him tensely. He was about as sure as I was. *I was going to blow this*.

There were 5 metres of crack to a ledge that would be my refuge, and 2 metres below me was the last piece of protection I had — a lonely mechanical device nestled insecurely in a flaring, tapered granite crevice that would hopefully be my saviour in case I did, in fact, bail.

I was trembling, my fingers were over-tightening with fear, and my exhausted legs were dancing around on footholds that were disappearing with every passing moment — my shaking limbs would have made Elvis proud. I tried as hard as I could to reach that ledge. I craned my neck, my back, my fingers, my mind willing the ledge closer with every ounce of strength I had. I turned my entire body sideways, stretching with all my might, my hands slick with sweat, as my feet scraped and skated at anything that would submit to a positive hold. Then I was off.

The fall, like all others, didn't hurt. I fell through empty air. What did hurt was the rope catching behind the crook of my knee and flipping me upside down, the friction from the speed, texture and stupidity burning my soft skin in a nice long line of searing pain across the back of my leg. This was, unfortunately, shortly to be the last of my worries. The last camming device I had placed in an attempt to protect myself decided it no longer had my life's preservation in mind, and just as I took a sharp breath, with a cracking noise, it popped cleanly from the crack where I had placed it. Now I really fell. Upside down. Hurtling towards the granite ramp leading towards the white-grey crack from which I had just not so gracefully exited. The impact knocked the wind from me, the granite rock face ripping the ass out of my pants, slashing the skin from my cheeks, and possibly fracturing my tailbone, not to mention all in all just generally scaring the living daylights out of me.

For a moment I just hung there, upside down, in silence. My un-helmeted head was resting against the slab as

I hung suspended from my hips, my harness digging deeply into my skin. With adrenaline slowly surging through my body, I went into recovery mode. I assessed the initial damage first. I started from my ankles, making slow circles; there was movement and no pain ... check. Next my knees. I could feel long superficial rope burn ... check. My legs were structurally fine, so I worked my way up. My butt and lower back felt like a cricket bat had just been used in a futile attempt to realign my spine. I wiped a butt cheek and was surprised at the blood on my hand. I carried on my checks, and in a voice three octaves higher than normal, yelled down to Danny that I was okay and proceeded to right myself so there was no more blood running into my brain.

Apart from being shaken, exhausted, and still scared, I was relatively unscathed besides the aching tailbone and lower back pain. I looked at the cam that now hung loosely on the rope in front of me, twisted, lobes spinning and wires no longer where they should have been. Useless. I clipped it back onto my harness where it belonged, stretched my neck from side to side, took a long, deep breath, and looked up.

We had to make a decision. A hundred metres above us was the top of the cliff. I could hear the hikers talking and laughing. From there it was a casual but steep descent, an hour's hike back to the van. On the other hand, from our current position, hundreds of metres from the valley floor, it was a long, arduous task of rappelling down the cliff face, traversing slippery terrain, and locating suitable anchors or leaving expensive gear, not to mention it was a process that would take hours. It really wasn't a difficult decision. Going up was the only sensible option.

Adrenaline still coursed through my veins. I started a serious mental battle within myself. I had to do this so we could get out. But that fall had just scared the absolute living fuck out of me. I was hurting. I was wrecked, completely unsure if I could actually manage the moves, and I had just broken my main piece of protection to 'stop' what had just happened from happening again.

I yelled down to Danny. He was shaken as well as I had just thrown him into the wall with my fall, taking a chunk of skin off his elbow. So, I hung there, doubting, assessing, scheming. I don't know how long it took for me to find the willpower to attempt it again. I checked with Danny that he was holding the weight. Eventually I pulled up on the rope, my back hurting, my heart racing and my fingers still jittery. I removed any extra pieces of protection below me that I could spare and slowly jugged my way up the rope. I rested another minute, inhaled, exhaled, sucked in as much fresh air as I could. I shook my arms loosely behind my back, one by one dipping them into the chalk bag that hung loosely just above my blood-covered butt. Then, just as the pain started boiling up from my lower torso, I summoned every bit of energy and courage I had and surged upwards.

I jammed, crimped, smeared, pushed and pulled myself upwards with just my hands and feet. I twisted my sore and bloody knuckles into the rattling, flared cracks. I dug my toes into any weakness, twisting them, pushing with my toes, my ankles and my knees. I could feel the determination in my eyes, my vision narrowing. I was going to crush every single thing I grabbed with the force of a thousand men. I grit my teeth and, with a growl, pushed higher.

I reached a weakness in the rock, twisting my fingers into

a fissure with one hand as I frantically searched for a piece of protection on my harness with the other. I only had three pieces: one was broken, and when it came to the other two, neither of them fit. I decided on the better of the two and stuffed it into the rock in earnest, the overwhelming surge of blood filling my exhausted forearms that were becoming more and more useless with every passing second. I'd convinced myself that the piece was good as I watched two of the four cam lobes tip out and the whole thing rattle menacingly. If I slipped and this one blew, well, I didn't even want to think about it.

Twisting, reaching, pushing, feet skating on the polished rock face, fingers slipping on every hold as I passed the place I had fallen only minutes earlier, the pain and memory still fresh in my mind, the danger and consequences had never been more real. The ledge edged closer with every surge of willpower fed by something deep inside me. I thought I'd given it all before, but this was something else. Now I pushed harder, dug deeper, and literally gave it everything I had. My entire body shook as my hands, somehow powered by my now useless forearms, finally grabbed that ledge. With one last surge from an empty tank, I dragged my body over the ledge and slid seal-style across it. As I clipped the rope through the anchors and put Danny on belay by tying a support rope around a rock, tears ran down my face, and a devilish laugh burst from my parched lips. For a moment I rested my head against the warm granite, comforting myself. After a few moments passed and the tears dried on my dirty cheeks, I poked my head over the cliff, looked Danny in the eyes and yelled, 'Up is the only way out!'

A Reckoning Among the Rainbow Trout

MEGHAN E. BUTLER

I never liked fishing; the no-talking mandate confounded me. My father would take me to the lakeshore to toss lines but, within five minutes, I would break the deafening silence with absentminded chatter only to be admonished with a 'Tsk, tsk, you'll scare the fish.'

I was a tomboy with a half dress, the kind that allowed for my favourite shorts and a significant layer of dirt but still satisfied my mother's notion of the feminine ideal. If she wanted me to be a frilly girl, she shouldn't have cut my hair into a gender-neutral mullet. One day I had pigtails, the next I looked like the tow-headed version of Pat from *Saturday Night Live*. I don't remember what I did to deserve that, but I'm sure it wasn't pretty.

I wasn't the easiest child.

Both my parents are only children, and as their only child, we have no siblings or cousins to counterbalance my 'spirit'. My parents have always carried the burden.

Years later I would learn that various counsellors and well-meaning friends told my parents my outrageous bull-headedness and big personality would serve me well. Now they tell me they can see the pay off.

I'm still trying to see it.

What no one told them was how lonely it would make me in the meantime.

Put me in a situation where I'm not allowed to talk, even if I have nothing to say, and I will become unglued. The idea that my very humanity is being stifled, that my ability to connect is being denied, is unbearable.

This is probably my natural resting state of loneliness-induced talking. I walk about the world with the deepest need for meaningful connection.

'Taking a fish', or sitting in a deer blind together, was quality time with my father. Both options unsettled me for a simple reason: for two people who enjoy each other's company so much, how could my father have nothing to say?

As a socially taxed adult, I now understand his truth. It's not that he had nothing to say, it's that he needed a break from saying.

I have a long-held fear of shared silence instigated by another. I fear it means something — a rift, a vast indifference, a dislike — when it rarely means anything at all. I so easily forget that someone else might be stuck in their own head, much like I am in mine; that they can enjoy breathing the same air without talking through it.

But it took me decades to figure that out.

As equal parts of both of my parents, I toggle between their extremes. I seek quiet alone time. Perhaps too much. Like my father. But then I come alive in social engagements and human connection. Like my mother.

This makes the idea of dating problematic. Finding my person requires a certain dedication and finesse for which I have little patience or social energy. It's taxing, more so, even, than the strain of staying quiet on the banks of a river.

This makes me wonder how my parents did it.

Did my fun-loving, gregarious mother, a classic sport dater herself, suffer so much social trauma through her own failed attempts that by the time my introverted-but-charismatic father showed up in their Sunday School class, she thought, 'Bingo!'?

Do they know now how squarely I fall in the middle of their shared social spectrum? My need for connection or disconnection swinging as widely as my casting line?

My greatest social struggle is my need to connect with someone else meaningfully, but in a way that doesn't send me to a dark cave for three days.

By following my profession in public relations — the very definition of social connection and influence — and my evolution into emotional intelligence development in leadership, I have perhaps found my solution.

To become the most useful version of myself, I must overextend into the unknown and the uncomfortable. To build stronger but moveable boundaries around myself, I must continue tearing down the old ones. And to accomplish all of this I must challenge what I've feared, and I've been doing this for as long as I can remember.

In an effort to rewrite the story of shared silence that I've always told myself, I sought an opportunity to take it seriously. To try and find this silent state of bliss through guided fly fishing.

I visited the Broadmoor's Fly Fishing Camp in Colorado, a historic grouping of cabins that have been lovingly restored for a sophisticated outdoor experience, complete with world-class hosts, fly-fishing experts, cuisine and adventure. As I wound my way through the Rocky Mountains towards Tarryall Creek, I had no idea what I had signed myself up for.

I was worried that I hadn't packed the right gear, or enough layers for the unpredictable mountain weather. I was terrified I would hook myself in the face in a clumsy attempt at casting. And I hoped I wouldn't pick up another expensive hobby, something I needed as much as another hole in my head.

But the root of my unease was wondering if I would survive hours on end not talking to the person standing next to me, whose job was to teach me how to fly fish.

THE. HORROR.

As is typical, most of the things I fear never actually happen.

My guide, the human equivalent of a golden retriever —
slightly shaggy, high energy and extroverted, who'd prefer
to be outside than in — was eager to tell me everything he
knows. There was no pretense. No awkwardness.

He showed me around the grounds and then immediately
ushered me into fishing waders, clunky, rubbery trousers
that looked familiar in the same way a wetsuit did, but
whose mechanics were totally foreign to me. I stealthily
watched as he donned his own gear. Then I silently copied
him.

By acting as if I knew what I was doing, I thought I might
actually fool myself into that reality. This strategy worked
for once. Within 30 minutes of my arrival, I was standing in
the middle of the river desperately hoping I wouldn't fall in
and that I would continue to look somewhat capable. That
I wouldn't be a screaming liability.

Then the unimaginable happened.

My guide started talking to me.

And never stopped.

For.

Three.

Days.

A professional fisherman and hunter, he had scaled the
Idahoan mountains alone in the middle of winter on an
elk hunt, just to carve it up and haul it out himself. He'd
fish in any body of water that would accept his line. He
was coming off a very quiet winter and wanted to enjoy

the company of his guests — fast and fleeting friends, a different set every few days.

Perhaps, like me, he just wanted to be heard. To be known and to know someone.

I didn't expect to catch a fish, much less a new pal.

By simply being myself and following the energy of the moment and of the water, and by taking his instructions and not getting in the way of it, I caught monster trout. One after another after another. I clumsily held them and thanked them and then gingerly placed them back in the current.

He taught me a new artform, not a sport.

After listening to his stories, I realized I want to be known by someone like he knows the wild.

He knows every bend in his river. He knows where the currents meet and where they break. He knows exactly how much rain will cause the waters to turn and toil and breech the banks. He knows how many days of enduring and unseasonable heat will choke his waters.

He knows every rock around which the trout tuck themselves away, lazing in a pocket of optimal coolness and oxygenation. He knows by smelling the air and looking under a rock which of the day's insects will delight his fish and those that are entirely insignificant.

He knows his rainbow trout. He doesn't just catch and release them. He handles them with grace and respect. He feels deeply if he should inadvertently harm one or cause it any kind of stress. He cares so much that, shockingly, he fishes without a hook.

And from the banks of the river to its deepest fishing holes, he remains pathologically optimistic that the next cast will be *the* cast, the one whose force threatens to upend him in his waders.

The gift of his conversation while fishing together meant more to me than the brief moment in which I perfected a long cast.

Now I was the one who needed the quiet time.

As I drove away in restorative silence through the Continental Divide, I realized I've always joked about being a 'fisher of men'. It turns out that perhaps I'm the beautiful and elusive rainbow trout just waiting for the attentive fisherman to cast his line in my direction.

Hopefully, he won't throw me back in silence.

The Secret of the Fearless

TARA GOLDSMITH

The idea of spending sixteen hours on a plane filled me with dread, but the desire to see Taroko Gorge in Taiwan was greater than any fear of flying I had. I've been travelling to different parts of our planet, facing my fears head-on, having developed my own survival technique without paying for any overpriced fear-of-flying courses. Self-help books were a great inspiration for various techniques, but they had all been futile. A list of ten things you see on the plane while worrying about crashing was far-fetched, as the only thing you can see is cloud, an engine, and stewards running up and down the aisle, while the main thought in your burning brain is when they are going to announce an emergency. But I liked the idea of writing a memoir on a ten-hour long-haul flight and went through lengthy preparations to find the perfect notebook with the right soft cover and smooth paper and the right pen. It had to be metal, black and light in the hand. I wanted it to be stylish, like my life.

Once high in the air, it dawned on me that I was too young to write a memoir. My life hasn't been like those of WAGS who squeeze twenty years into 120 pages. My memoir would probably fill ten pages and be double-spaced with a 14-font size. Someone suggested learning a new language, and I have always been fascinated with Chinese. It sounded right, but not on an Air China flight to Beijing where rows of friendly Chinese passengers are trying to teach you how to pronounce *ni hao* (hello). The fact that they all come from different parts of China and don't have the same dialect, let alone accent, made me very agitated, confined to my own seat with headphones and anxiety as long as a ten-hour flight to Beijing.

Frustrated, I developed my own technique, which was very simple: get drunk by the time you get to the airport, lay low while you pass through security and passport checks, then find a quiet corner in the least popular place that serves alcohol and get more courage down your throat before boarding the plane. On the way to the boarding gate, say a prayer, make the sign of the cross a few times and fall asleep by the time the plane takes off. A very good plan with certain limitations due to the alcohol absorption. It works for the first eight hours of your long-haul flight, until you suddenly feel wide awake with a huge hangover and massive disorientation over the middle of Siberia, wondering where the nearest exit is — just in case.

In order to avoid a similar situation in the future, I managed to get sleeping pills from my doctor, citing very bad nerves when flying. He was very considerate and gave me a prescription for tablets strong enough to tranquilize a horse, let alone a healthy young woman. So, when alcohol stopped its magic, I would take the pills. And my DIY technique worked!

Being incredibly pedantic, I also carry my last wishes neatly written down in my diary. When I found out that most plane accidents involve fire and burning, I began recording my messages on my phone. Those messages would change from flight to flight as life would change. On one flight I would leave everything to my current boyfriend but on the next, taken a mere four weeks after the last recorded message, I would leave everything to my sister. My biggest fear was not death itself but death in a foreign country and in a plane crash. The idea of having a burial ceremony of your phone because that would be the only part left of you, right?

On the flight to Taipei, I didn't re-record any messages or write down any last wishes as my colleague, Rachel, was laughing at my obsessions, even though she was more nervous about flying than me. But she believed in some wristbands bought on the Internet, which were supposed to reduce her fear of flying by touching them.

Taroko Gorge, which in the Truku language used by the indigenous people in the area, means 'magnificent and splendid', was exactly that and no more needs to be said. The additional treat was the autumn weather, which was not too hot and not too cold, but perfect for a visit. The return to Taipei was scheduled on a 45-minute flight. Again, I didn't record my messages. Why should I? I had had a nice time in a very nice place, with very nice people, nice food, and nice weather. Everything was just nice. It seemed like my obsession had disappeared. I didn't feel the need to get drunk or to take sleeping tablets.

While waiting at the gate, I had a terrible feeling that the plane, a Boeing 737, was too big for a short flight and only a handful of passengers. That was my inner frequent flyer talking, but then I dismissed my thoughts as due to a lack of alcohol. We took off nicely, and I glued my face to the window admiring the gorges from above. I was happy on a plane without any props for the first time, and I even refused alcohol. Sitting comfortably and thinking how flying can actually be pleasant, I suddenly heard a loud scream coming from Rachel. She turned to me with her big, black eyes and shouted, 'We are going down!' I ignored her.

The plane made a little clatter like the last coin in a tin box. Having been almost paralyzed, I turned my attention to the window. The blue sky was beautifully covered in scattered white clouds with strong rays of sunshine piercing through them. Then there was an eerie silence. We weren't flying. We were gliding through the clouds. The pilot was switching off both engines hoping to restart them again to gain altitude.

My inner intrepid was at peace. If I had to die in a plane crash, let it be here with these beautiful clouds and sunshine without any alcohol and tablets. The idea of having a proper burial with all my friends and family disappeared. My short and memorable life didn't flash in front of my eyes, and I wasn't saying goodbyes to any members of my family. I just stayed still, not worrying about anything and enjoying the brightness shining in through the window.

By this time there was a lot of commotion while Rachel's screams were broken by the engine rattling. It sounded like my aged Ford Fiesta on a cold winter's day mixed with my loud swearing. At some point the pilot gave up on having both engines on and decided to land the plane with one engine. He did it without a glitch, and the ten of us clapped and cheered. Rachel was crying.

Once safely on the tarmac, the full extent of the danger we had been in hit me hard. Having seen the number of ambulances and fire engines parked next to the plane made me realize how close we were to crashing. On the return flight from Taipei to London, I duly reinstated my ritual — alcohol, sleeping tablets and a little more alcohol with last wishes duly recorded. These days the flight from Taroko Gorge to Taipei is taken by a twin-engine plane. Rachel is happy to take short-haul flights, without a wristband but with sleeping tablets.

On Driving (and Dining) Alone

CHRISTINA MYERS

The third time the engine died, I was on a hill. I let the truck coast through the darkness, a heavy dread settling in my chest. I'd gotten lucky the first two times, but the chances of starting the truck again, with nothing but fumes now left in the gas tank, were slim at best.

Snow was falling harder by the minute; the blacktop of the narrow country road (which had seemed a major route connecting two freeways when I'd charted my trip from the foldout map), was visible only in patches through the blanket of white.

I'd managed to ignore the worry that had been brewing in the back of my head, focusing instead on watching my speed, keeping the windows defrosted, and checking the map every few minutes. But my fear bloomed fully now, a panicked litany inside my head: *Why did you do this? Why did you come alone? Why did you insist on taking this route?* And, most urgently: *What are you going to do?*

I tapped the brakes as the hill stretched out into a long, low curve, though I hated to lose speed. Logically, it didn't really matter if the truck died here or a little further up the road, but instinct wanted me to put off the inevitable as long as possible. Eventually, I was going to be stranded in the middle of nowhere, alone in the dark, slowly being buried by snow.

✳ ✳ ✳

There's one primary route to travel from Vancouver to the town of Nelson in the Kootenay region of British Columbia: head east roughly parallel to the Canada–US border on Highway 3, known as the Crowsnest. There's another route, circling further north through the interior then back down, but it's a longer albeit easier drive. Both roads are busy and well-maintained.

But after studying the map, I'd decided that it would be more *interesting* to travel to my friend's house in Nelson by first heading south into the US, then travelling east through Washington State, and re-entering Canada at one of the border crossings just south of my destination. Instead of powering through in a single day, as I would have on Highway 3, I'd turn it into a two-day journey with an overnight pit-stop in the tourist-friendly town of Leavenworth. The route was several hundred miles long, much of it through unpopulated forest, over a high mountain pass — and I'd be doing it in November in an old Mazda stick-shift pickup.

That this seemed like a good idea can be blamed superficially on my optimism and innocence and a family penchant for road trips off the beaten path but, more realistically, it was the fact that I was eighteen and eager to be away from complicated dramas at home, even if only briefly.

✳ ✳ ✳

The first day's travel was lovely: cold and crisp with clear blue skies all the way south along Interstate 5, with a few clouds and light snow as I turned eastward on Highway 2, heading inland. I had a stack of mixed tapes and listened to them one by one, thrilled by the solitude. I made Leavenworth in good time and checked into a motel.

I stretched out on the bed like a starfish, pleased by the luxury of a queen-size bed compared to my little twin trundle at home. I flipped on the TV, browsed the channels until I found *Jeopardy*, and lay back on a stack of pillows. I was, definitely, absolutely, without a doubt, very grown up now.

At 6:00 p.m., I changed into a black velvet dress and tights, tucked a book into my purse, and asked for dinner recommendations at the front desk. The clerk wrote instructions on a scrap of paper: go out the front door, turn left, go up two blocks. There I would find a quiet and cozy Italian restaurant.

'Wonderful, thank you,' I said, pleased at my poise and maturity. But as I walked, what had been a perfectly rational and very mature idea while alone in the hotel room seemed suddenly ridiculous. The restaurant was beautiful; not big-city fancy, but small-town cozy with candlelight and white tablecloths and brown leather menus with gold tassels. Standing in its foyer, I felt five years old.

'Table for one, please,' I said.

I'd intended to sound sophisticated, but instead my voice was shaky. I tugged at my dress, pulling the hem down, and swayed from foot to foot, unaccustomed to the high heels. I wished I'd stayed in the hotel room watching *Jeopardy*. But I was committed now; I'd simply have to fake my way through it.

∗ ∗ ∗

This wasn't my first solo trip. The summer prior I'd borrowed my Mom's car and gone camping for several days, and I had friends living all over the region that I'd often go visit for a night or two. I soon got a taste for disappearing here and there and was vague with friends if they asked where I'd been. I planned a trip overseas with someone for the following year, but when they could no longer go — and assumed I'd cancel, too — I re-imagined it as a solo journey and bought my train ticket as a single.

I loved everything about travelling alone, which was counterintuitive, as most of the time I was an extrovert who craved the energy of other people. But it turned out that I was good at being alone too. It took me by surprise, this unexpected satisfaction I discovered in getting myself lost and then unlost, packing just enough to get me through, listening to good music along a stretch of highway with no one else in the car. To this day, even after years of marriage and motherhood, I still get a particular thrill when I put a single suitcase in the trunk of my car.

* * *

I ordered a Caesar salad and pasta, and when they brought the bread, I pulled my book out of my purse. Was it a *faux pas* to read at the table in a fancy restaurant? Was it acceptable since I was alone and young? I didn't know the answer, but I felt foolish sitting here alone, staring around the room at the other patrons, all of them in pairs and foursomes, while my hands fiddled with my skirt under the table. *Travelling alone* was an invisible activity, but I hadn't anticipated that *eating alone* came with an audience. I was out of place and anxious to be done with the entire episode.

I pretended I was utterly at ease, chatting with the waiter and smiling as people passed by my table. I don't know if I was a good actress or if my naïve performance inspired sympathy, but at the end of the meal my waiter brought out a piece of cheesecake, *on the house*.

'From the chef, to thank you for joining us this evening,' he said, formally and sincerely. 'Don't rush,' he added. 'Enjoy.'

I was delighted. And addicted. I added eating alone to my list of solitary pleasures.

* * *

It's a strange sound, the noise that a truck makes when it's still moving but there's no rumble from the engine. As the truck coasted, I could hear the creak of the metal frame and the tap-tap-tap of the passenger seatbelt flapping against the door. My fingers gripped the steering wheel tighter, my palms sweaty despite the cold, my stomach fluttering with adrenaline as I watched the highway illuminate 30 feet at a time in front of my headlights. All around me the world was inky darkness, punctuated here and there by the sparkle of the moon on snow-crusted branches.

This is it! I'm going to be stranded in the middle of nowhere! I thought, the long hill flattening out, my speed dropping off quickly now, rounding a last, slow curve. But as I came around the hillside, a glow appeared. Ahead of me was a small crossroad, a single flashing red light and green highway direction signs.

And a gas station.

I gasped, a desperate sound even to my own ears, and then choked out a half-cry half-laugh. I coasted into the parking lot and absurdly, impossibly, magically, rolled right up to the pump.

* * *

I made it to my friend's house in Nelson by dawn, and four days later, after a handful of misadventures, headed back home via the Crowsnest Highway. I should have been fearful, watching the sky for signs of bad weather, stopping at each small town for another top-up of gas, eager only to be home safe and sound.

But I was invincible now: I'd coasted into a gas station in the middle of nowhere with a dry tank. I'd driven through a snowstorm, across the mountains, through the border and back. And I'd taken myself out for a fancy dinner in a velvet dress and eaten dessert by candlelight — and survived.

The world was waiting for me, and I was ready.

Snapper in Essaouira

CALLUM BROCKETT

We ate red snapper with our fingers. It sat in foil on Erin's lap, oil and lemon juice sliding down her leg. We tore off bits of white flesh from the bones as the red scales lined with charcoal crackled under our greasy fingers. The sun hid behind grey clouds, and the sea, churned by the constant wind, was a dark and angry green. In front of us stretched a rocky, moss-covered beach that clashed with the Atlantic Ocean. On our left, the Essaouira Citadel stood tall along Scala Harbour. On our right were the cramped and cracked buildings of the Medina.

We enjoyed the ocean spray, even if the brilliant blues that had saturated online pictures of Essaouira had been sapped from view. We had spent weeks moving inland, towards the south-eastern entrance of the Sahara Desert, before doubling back towards Morocco's coast. The bus rides were cramped and warm, the winding High-Atlas roads nauseating. But now a breeze carried saltwater instead of sand, and Essaouira had more in common with a relaxing Greek Island town than the bustling hives of Marrakech and Fez.

That morning, we had met Abdul. He ran the hostel we had booked, which sat deep within the Medina. The green, milky doors, which had cracked from too much time in the wind, were its only distinguishing feature. Abdul welcomed us with mint tea; there was never any shortage of mint tea in Morocco.

Abdul gave us maps of the city and rattled off a list of things to do. He highlighted the cafés and restaurants we should visit.

'But, if you want the best, most fresh fish, you go here,' he said, pointing to the pier on the map. 'The fish market. A must. Fresh fish caught daily. The stalls in the Medina will grill it for you.'

'Is it cheap?' I asked, unable to help myself.

'Maybe not for you,' Abdul said with an embarrassed chuckle. 'But you might get lucky.'

Abdul picked up the copper teacups and placed them on a tray.

'A warning. Be wary of the fisherman.'

'Why is that?'

He looked down at the teacups in his hands. His smile vanished. Abdul hesitated, as if having to dislodge the word from between his teeth.

'Heroin.'

'Heroin?'

'Yes. There is not much work for the fishermen now. They trade the drug among themselves in the coves of the fortress wall. The town continues to grow with all you beautiful visitors. But not for them. They have been fisherman their whole lives, and now there is nothing for them.'

'That's so sad,' Erin said. I nodded in agreement. It's all we can offer.

The pier sat across from the Citadel, stretching out beyond the cluster of stalls, all with large stands of fish sitting by their side. All the stalls used the same blue-and-white-striped plastic chairs and tables. We tried to be polite as we pushed away the menus. One stall worker told Erin how beautiful she was, and another swore his grill was the best in Morocco. We pushed through, making our way to the sea-soaked pier.

The larger fishing boats were berthed in the harbour, their masts and rigging creating a rusty web. Many boats had been pulled from the water and stranded on slates. Barnacles and moss choked the stripped hulls with woven fenders and fishing nets left dangling on the bow. Men gathered around great masses of crustaceans, fish and eels. An unrelenting sea spray meant the fishermen had given up trying to stay dry. The sun still had not come out to offer any warmth. Young men sat huddled in jeans and Adidas jumpers, while elders wore *djellabas*: a loose, striped cloak that trailed through the puddles of seawater. Eyes followed us as we walked along the pier. I felt Erin draw closer.

We were determined to buy our dinner from the market

and not give in to the convenience of a restaurant in the Medina. The bullish hustle disappeared as we walked along the pier, deep stares replacing the compliments and boastful claims. I got that all-too-familiar feeling of being somewhere I shouldn't be. English was lost the further we went ventured, and neither of us spoke any French or Arabic. As a wave broke against the sea wall and our socks soaked through, we went to find our dinner.

We inched closer to the mounds of sea life, but still, the fisherman gave us nothing except their salty stares. Abdul's warning was fresh in my mind, our hands stuffed deep in our pockets. Blood and fish guts moved through the puddles of seawater, flowing out over the pier, returning the innards to the ocean. It felt strange to grow hungry amongst the strong smell of fish, with nothing to stare at but the splayed carcasses, skinned and skewered. We fought the urge to turn back towards the comfort of the tourist crowds and busy restaurants.

One fisherman caught my attention. His eyes locked with mine, and he gruffly pulled on his hair, smiling as he did so. Most Moroccan men kept their hair cropped short, but this one's extended past his ears, each strand dry and tangled by the salty wind. My own hair sat around my shoulders. I smiled back at him.

The fisherman's stand was small and lined only with the same red fish. If the sun had been out, I imagined the scales would have glittered with silver streaks. I pointed to the fish and held up a single finger. He smiled, touched his hair again and pulled the largest fish from the stand. He held up three fingers. Thirty dirham. I looked at Erin, and she shrugged her shoulders.

After he handed me the bagged fish, he extended his arms, held out his fingers and clapped them together, like an animal gnashing its jaws. He also snapped with his teeth and laughed as we jumped.

'Snapper,' he said, his own jaw coming apart and revealing bare gums.

'Snapper,' I repeated and offered a shaky laugh in return.

As we turned to leave, the long-haired fisherman held up another finger.

'Were you looking to have a good time tonight?' Each word was muffled. He had to repeat himself, so I could understand. He pulled out a small bag of white powder.

I did my best to laugh again.

'Just the fish, thanks.'

The fisherman looked at me, confused. He didn't speak English. He had memorized those words and those words alone. I wondered in how many different languages he spoke that same phrase.

I shook my head, held up the fish and nodded. He returned the nod. He waved goodbye, sat back in a puddle of seawater and blood, and placed the small bag in his pocket.

Having the fish cooked at one of the blue-and-white stalls only cost another 30 dirham. It wasn't much to pay for a fish that this morning had been alive, battling the currents of the Atlantic. We felt proud of the catch, as if we alone had pulled the snapper from the roiling waves.

A crowd gathered along the city walls, all hopeful of a spectacular sunset, but the sun still hid behind heavy clouds. A man traversed across the rock pools that crowded the beach, jumping from one rock to the next, becoming slightly more unbalanced with every leap. A band played behind us and people danced in the main square. The call to prayer came and went, but the fishermen continued to pack up their mounds of fish and place oars in the smaller blue rowboats.

The man on the rock pools began to dance. It was violent dancing, quickly moving his hands among the sand, then abruptly offering them to the sky. He stumbled and fell but managed to pull himself from the rock pools' stagnant waters. I realized it was the fisherman who had sold us our red snapper, sand now clinging to his shaggy curls. The crowd murmured and let out muffled, embarrassed laughs. A few tourists clapped, but the dancing did not stop, and we all tried to focus on something else. I felt uneasy, being part of the unappreciative audience.

The fisherman then fell again and lay kneeling over with his head pressed against the sand. It looked as if he had washed ashore with the high tide and had been left to wither away in the wind. The grease from the snapper lingered on my lips, and the lemon felt harsh on my tongue. Only the snapper's skeleton remained.

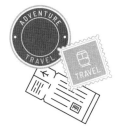

Trespassing in Tanzania

SINÉAD MCWEENEY

Laughter rings out like tinkling bells, a rich, sweet sound that sends warmth seeping into my heart. Mild, sweaty incense pervades the room as the girls trickle into the shelter from the dense, dusty Tanzanian air outside. Their eyes are bright like candles, burning and curious as they drink in the sight of a *mzungu*, a white person, me. My chest tightens under their expectant gaze.

Aunt Rachel hands me a Bible with a nod and a smile, and I force my lips into a brief boomerang shape before letting them fall back to a tense line. A few days before my eighteenth birthday, I had embarked on my first solo international flight, taking me from Dublin to Paris, Nairobi, Dar es Salaam and finally, Mwanza. Having distant family members meeting me at the end of my 40-hour journey from home was a comfort, but it didn't stop images of my plane plummeting 35,000 feet into a Saharan sand dune tormenting my brain for weeks before my flight. Nor did it calm my panic at sleeping on a brown and yellow stained mattress under a ripped mosquito net and a squeaky fan; or prevent my shrieks of terror as potentially sickness-carrying tsetse flies sunk their teeth into my skin while I tried to sleep. Now, however, I came face to face with an unanticipated fear, its sneering smirk quickening my heartbeat, its suffocating embrace forcing a glossy sheen of perspiration to break out across my skin.

The Bible is heavy in my hands as I flick through its thin pages, avoiding the eyes of everyone in the room, suddenly hyper aware of every passing motorbike outside and the shuffle and squeak of the desks in front of me. I don't want to be just another white girl spending a few hours in a shelter for street kids, tell them everything's alright when it's not, then taking a photo and leaving — just another blow-in from Europe exacting a high of self-righteousness from 'helping' abandoned kids. My hands begin to tremble.

I stand next to Carol, the founder of the shelter. She nods, her brown eyes silently offering encouragement.

Together, we read Psalm 91 in Swahili. I follow the words in my English version. My heart clenches as they read, 'You will not fear the terror of night ...' We proceed to the end of the psalm and the girls are quiet. Contemplative. Remembering?

I wonder how I can stand here and teach wild fearlessness, unbridled freedom, inexplicable peace. Me, a sufferer of anxiety! Me, a rich, white girl who has never known hunger, thirst, entrapment. Me! I feel utterly unworthy.

My gaze runs over the faces of these girls, some my age, some as young as thirteen. There is Kelly, who aspires to become a journalist, despite having been forbidden to return to school by law since giving birth to her daughter a few years ago. There's Febe, who escaped a forced marriage with her children, only to find herself struggling to survive on the streets and now battling a painful illness. There are former prostitutes, rape survivors, child brides, HIV sufferers, mothers, sisters, friends, daughters. I see their precious, broken, golden hearts inside their chests yearning for real love, real joy, real peace. I am disconcerted by their silence.

Aunt Rachel's words emerge from the mire of my surging thoughts. It is not with my own authority that I can teach this wild assurance. 'The Lord says, "... I will be with them in trouble. I will rescue and honour them ..."' Whether one is a person of faith or not, there is something beautiful and golden about the eternal words of a Higher Power that is loving and kind and frustratingly difficult to understand. I picture the Father figure of God, not seated upon a lofty throne in heaven above, but weeping next to his daughter, His heart breaking at her suffering and offering a gentle embrace of comfort.

The class is dismissed, but the girls' eyes don't leave me. Part of me wants to jump into Aunt Rachel's car and return to my guesthouse back in the city, hiding behind my eyelids on my little sponge bed. I have a feeling that my time isn't yet done here.

Eager voices suddenly erupt and the floodgates open. The shy, giggling girls who tie-dyed material with me earlier have been forgotten, and they suddenly pool around me, reaching out and touching my pale skin, comparing my pallor to their rich cocoa tone. Their voices rise, a hybrid melody of Swahili and English weaving throughout the throng of bodies. Kelly translates for the girls who strain to understand my quiet English and becomes my right-hand lady. I'm questioned and interrogated like a celebrity, but I feel right at home.

I'm an introvert, awkward in crowds and uncomfortable in social situations, but here I feel somehow refreshed and invigorated. We live worlds apart. My hardships pale in comparison to theirs. Our stories lead us each down separate and wildly different paths, yet, we are all here together at this moment, and I feel a bond form. We're just a group of teenage girls chatting, giggling and getting to know each other. Accepting each other.

Mary retrieves her cracked and dented smartphone from her bedroom, thrusts her newborn into my arms and begins snapping. Thus begins the photo shoot. We pose in our khanga skirts and bare feet, babies on our hips like accessories.

I am still concerned. I fear for their safety once they leave the shelter in a few months. I feel my heart momentarily stop as I hope and pray for their happiness. I long for them to discover the beauty in this world, not denying the ugliness they have been unjustly exposed to but finding joy in spite of it. We have had fun today, and we have become friends in a way I didn't expect. I saw myself in them, and maybe they saw themselves in me. Fear is an obstacle to be overcome in every opportunity worth taking. I didn't, couldn't, overcome fear alone. These precious, golden-hearted, wide-smiling girls beckoned me beyond it and showed me how to laugh without fear of the future.

The Wrath of Whakaari

ANGIE BELCHER

Whakaari, or White Island, as named by Captain James Cook in 1769, loomed on the horizon like a steaming, freshly baked loaf of bread, appearing and disappearing beneath huge, billowing puffs of vapour. Its haunting shape has long beaconed adventurers, the most recent being us, kayakers, who have long dreamed of paddling the 50-kilometre stretch of water from Whakatāne to Whakaari, as named by Māori voyagers who paddled their huge *waka* (canoes) to the island in search of tasty mutton birds which inhabited the island in their thousands.

However, for some of us the distance is beyond our kayaking capabilities and, instead, we board a modern *waka*, a 17-metre launch piled high with colourful kayaks. Our goal is to circumnavigate Whakaari — it is a trip for the intrepid and the tireless, for those with arms like tree stumps and biceps as hard as rocks.

Conditions were good; the notorious Whakatāne Bar

was in a passive mood and the required permits to visit the privately owned island had come through at the last moment. We eased the launch through the maze of rocks, which punctuate the flow of water where the Whakatāne River pours into the sea and said a quiet *karakia* (Māori prayer) to the bronze statue of Wairaka, the daughter of Toroa, the captain-navigator of the Mataatua *waka*, one of the seven great canoes which brought the Māori people to New Zealand shores.

From the bow of the boat, huge white plumes could be seen, a signal that the fires within Whakaari's belly still burn with legendary fury. We could distinguish the occasional blot of colour on the island's otherwise stark and featureless landscape. Bright green patches of ice plant defied nature by thriving in these barren conditions, while huge areas of white guano indicated the gannet nesting sites. Estimated to exceed 10,000 in number, the gannets nest and feed their young for months before heading out to sea. An eerie haze hung above the colony. Clouds of ammonium chloride formed due to the hydrochloric acid in the volcanic steam reacting with the ammonia from the guano. But the gannets are not alone here. More than 60,000 grey-faced petrels burrow into the island, laying their eggs and raising their chicks.

We approached the island from the southwest, where the sea has breached the crater wall and created a small bay aptly named Crater Bay, and carefully unloaded all kinds of kayaks from double Sea Bears to skittish slaloms.

Testing the waters, we made our way to the shore. Small rivulets of steaming water ran along rust-coloured canals and over oxide-red boulders into the ocean. There was concern that the acidic water run-off would eat into the kayak hulls, so after some adrenaline-charged discussion we slowly headed off.

It takes three hours of paddling to circumnavigate the island, and all the while its dark shadowy presence loomed over us, shrouding us in a cooling discomfort. As we paddled, the island changed from steep, stark, gouged-out landscapes to clumps of grotesque, distorted trees.

Around us schools of *kahawai* and *maomao* fish circled in tight balls, while gannets plunged into their midst, picking off the unlucky outsiders. Dolphins joined the frenzy, and the occasional fin of a more sinister species pierced the surface. The wider area is renowned for game fishing while waters closer to the island remain protected by New Zealand's Marine Reserve legislation. It's no wonder the marine life is so prolific — less than 8 kilometres to the west is the White Island Trench, at a staggering 1219 metres deep.

With tired arms and aching backs, we paddled to the point of departure, Crater Bay, where the collapsed volcanic rim opens to the centre of the island. The highest point, Mount Gisborne, a mere 321 metres above sea level, could be seen ahead, signalling it was time to explore on foot. Our crew had carried protective gear ashore for us. Neoprene booties were replaced with tramping boots and a breathing apparatus was donned as protection from the sulphuric gases which would otherwise scratch our throats and tear at our lungs.

We passed the decaying remains of the once-thriving sulphur refinery, the only indication of any human occupation. Established in the late 1800s, the remains of the sulphur works are a monument to the continual battle between humans and nature. The solitude, the haunting noises and the constant fear of living in such a volatile environment took their toll on the workers. In 1914 the island rebelled with great force, burying everything, including eleven miners, under metres of ash. The only survivor was 'Peter the Great', the mining company's cat.

The stark ruins are a haunting reminder of the destructiveness, unpredictability and devastating power of nature — monument to the wrath of Whakaari. Silently picking through the ruin, I wondered how often the miners must have gazed towards the mainland and craved the peace and comforts of home.

Near the main crater, our boots cracked through the lightly baked crust of ash, leaving lunar footprints, silent and still, stretching behind us across the forbidding landscape.

Not a word was spoken as we stood on the rim of the volcano, mesmerized by the white steam patterns, which drifted out of the otherwise sombre pit. A shift in the wind direction revealed a gaping hole with a steaming sea of boiling green water. It was deep, very deep, without a single sign of life. We sensed the force of nature. It was overpowering. Behind us the gaping fumarole of Noisy Nelly screamed like a dying banshee.

We recoiled in disgust as our nostrils caught a whiff of sulphuric-acid fumes. At last sanity took over. Standing on the edge of a volatile volcano is no place to be. We made our way back to the mothership and docked our small craft alongside. One by one they were hoisted on board and lashed into place.

In silence we left the island, tired, paddle-weary and touched by the overwhelming power of White Island.

On the Road to Panic

MEGAN DWYER

I'm riding on a bus to the small, quaint town of Errezil in northern Spain. To get here, you have to drive through narrow, nail-biting roads that traverse the mountain ridge. We're passing cascading cliff tops, which feature every shade of green imaginable, and the cold, fresh air is seeping into the vents of the bus. The birds are loudly announcing our arrival, and the cows are staring as we drive past. The bus is like every public transport bus, the upholstery has a faint old smell but is still comfy enough to fall asleep in if you're desperate. Every few minutes we catch a glimpse of a distant, quaint farmhouse, but for the most part we're the only civilization in sight. We're in the middle of nowhere, with failing phone reception — and we're all about to die.

At least, I think we're about to die. It's a conflicted emotion because Ed Sheeran and Justin Bieber's *I Don't Care* is crackling through the radio as I process my imminent death.

I'm at a party I don't want to be at.

As we navigate the winding road, we hit every tree we pass under. I panic at the sound of a stray twig peeling the paint from the roof of the bus. I'm trying to see as far into the distance as possible, trying to see road bumps and potholes the driver might miss, but there's fog surrounding us. Every corner is blind.

We can't have more than a few centimetres between us and a catastrophic drop off of the mountain we've spent so long valiantly climbing. The driver hasn't been able to stay on the microscopic path, so we've run into the sliver of grass on either side of the road more than a few times.

Everyone else on the bus is calm; some are even sleeping. I try to reassure myself that everyone else would be panicked if we were *really* about to die.

Abruptly, my stomach twists, and I'm back in the car. The red car that went too fast. Where I felt just as out of control. When the car didn't stop and the brakes didn't work and the tree was the only thing strong enough to stand up against us. I'm smelling the same burning brakes, only this time coupled with leaking petrol.

You know I love you, did I ever tell you? You make it better like that.

I start imagining how the bus will sound when it crashes. Crash? Shudder? No. *Shatter.* Definitely shatter, maybe even a skid and then a shatter. People think it sounds like a thump, but the loudest noise is the headlights smashing, the metal crumpling, the last scream the car can make.

I hear the red car skid. I look to my right and see him staring at me. Panicked. Apologetic. He tries the brakes and they fail. He tries to swerve through the corner. He knows, I know. No escape, no alternative route. Just a tree and a car — destined to be.

I clutch my seatbelt in my hand, checking it is secure, bracing for impact.

Five.

Four.

Three.

Cause I don't care when I'm with my baby, yeah, all the bad things disappear.

My best friend beside me has her eyes pinned closed — but she can sense I'm feeling anxious. She holds a hand out to me and I lightly grip it, careful not to squeeze too hard and alert her that I'm losing my mind.

Two.

One.

The headlights explode. Glass immediately pours down and mixes with the petrol and stormwater. I lurch forward. The airbags fail as we smash into the dashboard and wheel. I hear my knee crunch into the glovebox. I feel my collarbone snap into itself. Leaves slowly sprinkle the car in soot and debris. The tree heaves forward, then sways calmly in unison with the wind and rain. I can hear myself screaming at him: 'Get out! Get out!' I'm not considering he might not be able to peel himself from the steering wheel.

I can't feel the bus wobble anymore. I see a gush of people running towards us; they're screaming, but I can't hear them.

Finish my drink, say 'shall we dance?' Hell, yeah!

My eyes refocus and start darting toward every tree. In the years following, when people drive through this small village, there won't be any evidence of a bus accident. I expected the red car to have totalled the tree, for it to be cracked at the seams, completely in half, destroyed. It wasn't. I was hoping to see scars — there weren't any to find. No wood that had regrown out of shape or bark which shed slightly faster. It was just a tree. No trauma to hide, no trauma to bear.

I can deal with the bad nights. When I'm with my baby, yeah.

I work through my steps to prevent any further breakdown — deep breaths, closed eyes, activated senses. Touch, smell, taste, sound, feel. I am gripping my seatbelt with such ferocity it's cutting through my hands. I can smell the burnt tyres. I can feel the overworked and smoking-hot brakes under my skin. I'm sweating. It's already too late. I'm too worked up.

The tears are welling in my eyes. I start biting my cheeks and clenching my jaw and swallowing as much as I can. But they're breaking free and I'm breaking down. My shoulders are on fire and the adrenaline is so rife in my veins it's painful to sit still. I start rubbing my fingertips together, fidgeting my toes and manically moving my tongue side to side. I reposition myself to face the window and sit perfectly still — embarrassed and hoping no one can see me. I watch the bus teeter and threaten to topple. Any minute now, it has to fall from this cliff.

Read your lips, I'd rather kiss 'em right back, with all these people all around, I'm crippled with anxiety.

I recompose myself. The bus takes another corner. I crumble again.

I don't have any tissues, so my only option is to quietly sob as I listen to girls exclaiming, 'This is so scary! This road is so small.'

While I'm still fighting the onslaught of trauma, my best friend begins hysterically whacking my shoulder. She's mumbling something and hitting me to turn around. I'm certain she wants me to reveal my soaked eyes and panic, but I can't bear to drop the calm façade. I quickly glare at her, trying to entice her to stop making a scene. As I whip my head towards her, I catch sight of the vomit falling from her mouth onto my clothes.

Ooh, ooh, ooh, ooh, ooh, ooh (no)

My brain is frying itself now. I'm conscious not to move so the mix of paella, sangria and potato chips remains as contained as possible.

I pause. My brain halts its preparations. I blink. I breathe. Miraculously, I'm laughing. I'm uncontrollably shaking and numb to the sensation of the vomit on my skin, but I am laughing. My eyes split at the seams, shooting tears faster down my face. Caught now by my cheeks, the tears gloss over my rosy and uplifted face. The tears trickle into my mouth, directed by my dimples.

We glance at each other, despair and gratitude washing over our faces.

The bus keeps driving, and we keep rolling through the mountains. Covered in vomit and listening to my best friend sniffle as she holds back more, I return focus to my calming techniques. Her hands are equally drenched in vomit, yet my anxiety cannot help itself. The minute the bus putters through a bend, I instinctively grab her hand. We bind our slippery hands together, her other hand occupied with clutching a makeshift vomit bag, mine still glued to my seatbelt.

When we arrive safely at the farmhouse we are staying at, I find the driver, thank him for a safe arrival and excellent driving — and quickly mention that his seats might have some vomit on them.

Namibian Nights

HARRY CUNNINGHAM

At the risk of stating the obvious, the Namib Desert in Africa is vast, scorching hot, and largely devoid of life. In fact, the word *namib* in the local Khoekhoe language actually means 'vast', so you know I'm not lying. In the last 80 million years, just a handful of hardy animal species have been able to successfully adapt to the extreme conditions presented by this desert environment. So, you can imagine my dismay at finding out, on the eve of attempting to run through this desert, that lions were one of those species that could.

Whilst Namibian lions have found a way to thrive in the heat, I speak on behalf of all sweaty Homo sapiens when I say that we certainly have not. But that doesn't stop us from trying. Each year about 100 active-wear-clad (human) athletes attempt to race 250 kilometres across the oven-like Namib Desert on foot as part of the '4 Deserts Ultramarathon Series'.

I am three days into a race that has so far gifted to me throbbing knees, aching ankles, cracked lips, a pink neck, and quite a bit of thirst. The fourth day of the race is the one that I am most worried about — the notoriously physical and mentally draining 'Longest Day'. Aptly named, I have to traverse an unbroken 84 kilometres over sandy beaches, jagged shale mounds, gravel valleys, crusty salt-flats, dusty basins, imposing sand dunes and, of course, the hard-packed red dirt that is so characteristic of Africa, none of which are particularly pleasant to run on. It is almost twice as far as I have ever tried to run in one go before, and I have no idea how my body or mind will cope.

For all of my worries, the Longest Day starts relatively well. From the coast I sweep inland over a small rocky crest and into a wide, Martian valley that fan bakes me as I pass through. Although the temperatures shoot up well above 40 degrees Celsius before ten o'clock, I am puffing through the kilometres without too much incident. By contrast, just three days prior we were forced to divert our route to give a local pride of lions a wide berth, adding almost 10 extra kilometres early in the day. Namibian lions, we are told, can patrol an area up to 400 kilometres square, more than three times the size of San Francisco, so we have to make an effort to avoid straying too close. At the time, I don't think too much about it, and now, three days later, in the blinding sunlight and with a heap of distance ahead of me, desert lions are the least of my worries. My biggest problems are staying hydrated, avoiding blisters, and not damaging any important body parts (the less important ones I can sacrifice).

The day grinds on, and after about ten hours of slurping

electrolytes and shuffling across sunbaked surfaces, I have covered nearly 60 kilometres. This is now the farthest distance I have ever run in one go, something which my stabbing joints will not let me forget. I have spent more time on my feet than any other day so far, so when the 12-hour mark comes up, I am a little surprised to notice the temperature actually dropping. My shadow is lengthening toward the hills on my right. I no longer need my sunglasses, and the reality that I will soon be running in the dark occurs to me, absurdly, for the first time that day. I look around from horizon to horizon — not a body in sight. I am perhaps as isolated as I have ever been in my life, physically exhausted, emotionally drained, and suddenly very aware of my vulnerability to the great expanse of nature. The sun falls unstopping out of the sky. Darkness is looming.

The sun's inevitable disappearance below the horizon happens with at least five hours of running to go, and my entire world is reduced to a pitiful circle of light emanating from my headlamp onto the rugged ground in front of me. My stomach tightens, and unease creeps in. Whichever way I look I am met with an impenetrable blackness. I am entirely alone in a desert, in one of the least populated places in the world, and, it suddenly occurs to me, I am in lion territory.

As I remember this inconvenient fact, adrenaline floods through my body, my heart rate shoots up, and my aching limbs are temporarily forgotten. Where before I was met with pitch black, now I see lions everywhere, moving across the open plains alongside me, stalking me from behind, waiting ahead behind a rock. Lions mostly hunt at night,

I recall, and only roar when they have already fed. I hear no roars, so they must be hungry. I keep moving forward, following the faintly illuminated green glow sticks that mark the route, gripped by an inescapable fear of being pounced on at any moment. Left, right, left, right, stop. Look up. Turn a full circle. Squint. Listen intently. No lions. Keep going. Left, right, left, right. I feel like a child sprinting back into bed in the middle of the night after a trip to the bathroom, racing against an imagined intruder ready to jump out and grab me, only this feeling goes on and on for hours as I trudge deeper into blackness.

I have to keep my head pointed down at the ground so I don't roll my ankle on a rock, but I am sure that that is when the lions will choose to attack. I must keep moving; I have to get to the finishing line before they finish me off. How do you even fight off a lion? I rack my brains. Do I run at it screaming to try and scare it away? Or do I act submissive and hope it can't be bothered chewing the meagre amounts of meat off my bones? Maybe I can find a stick, or perhaps a big rock to deter its inevitable onslaught. Left, right, left, right.

More hours pass. I am so tired I want to cry; fifteen hours of non-stop running has taken its toll on my emotions. I have been baked alive, but now I am freezing cold and fleeing from at least 100 blood-thirsty lions. I have looked at nothing but my own feet and dusty rocks for the past three hours, which is mind-numbingly boring and driving me crazy. Did I mention there are at least 200 lions right on my tail? As exhausted and drained as I am, I try and inject more pace, ignoring my body's unanswered plea for mercy. Another hour moving, and then another. Left, right, left, right.

Finally, finally, I hear the drums. BOOM. BOOM. BOOM. BOOM. After near silence and total darkness for five hours, the drums beating at the finishing line are almost as scary as the lions that have surely been chasing me all night. Almost. It is 1:00 a.m., and I have been running for about 17 hours when I finally stumble into the light.

Cheers. Clapping. Drums. Fires. Tents. Snoring. Other humans! I am ecstatic. And woozy. A smile almost as wide as the Namib itself wraps its way across my face. I survived! Take THAT lions.

I collapse next to a burning brazier, attempting to peel off my shoes with one hand and rummaging into my food bag for a midnight snack of pain relief with the other. A couple of other competitors are cupping warm drinks while debriefing on their respective days, and as I struggle to wrest my shoes off my swollen feet, I ask if there is any word on the pride of lions that disrupted our first day of running.

'They moved off yesterday, apparently,' a slim, athletic Englishman who finished hours ago answers. 'Hundreds of kilometres away by now they reckon.'

'Not that it matters,' adds his friend. 'The lions here are pretty well-fed. They are the only lions in the world that hunt seals on the coast, and because they are relatively easy prey and very fatty, the pride never really goes hungry.'

I laugh, mostly at myself, and my hip flexors contract painfully. Of course, I was never in any danger of being eaten by lions. Why on earth would they let us run through the desert at night if they ever thought that could happen? In the light of camp and surrounded by people, it all seems so obvious, so stupid.

I finally shrug my second shoe off and inspect the damage to my feet. Quite a bit of skin has come off, and there is some blood in my sock from three or four blisters that have split open. That will need to be dealt with before I start day five tomorrow.

'Ouch, what happened to your feet mate? Looks like a lion got to them.'

Any Pub in a Storm

BARBARA COLE

At midnight, dressed for sleep in my navy-blue night dress and wool poncho, I drove into Radillo's Pub and Pool, a red cement building surrounded by a muddy parking lot. Hand-printed signs on the wall advertised Thursday karaoke night. Twice I had driven past, avoiding it. The fuel station where I had asked for directions and received an unhelpful reply was the only other place showing any sign of life in stormy Gonubie, South Africa.

I parked in the muddy lot, opened the door, snapped it shut again, reopened it and stepped into a mud puddle wearing my sandals. Mud all around, everywhere. There's no good way to step on mud. You put one foot on it. You sink. Oozy. There was rain and the wind howled. It was a miserable night by standards anywhere.

Walking in, dim lighting let me see five young to middle-aged white men huddled together. Four sat drinking on one side of the bar. The bartender, on the other side of the makeshift, wooden slab, gripped his own beer. Surprised at my presence, they glanced at me, then continued to drink.

One beer drinker asked where my husband was. 'Unsure,' I said. 'Haven't seen him in 30 years.' Laughing loudly, they continued to drink.

The day had been a long one, travelling from north of Durban through blinding rain. Slowing to 60 kilometres an hour, I screeched when a flock of sheep crossed the road, missing them by mere centimetres. Yes, a fricking flock of sheep — where was their dog? Where was their shepherd? I missed a straggling lamb by barely a tyre mark. Highways, even double lane freeway types, in this part of South Africa often have no fences. Animals wander freely at will. For some reason, their 'will' often seems more interesting on the opposite side of the road.

Every part of my concentration had been on keeping the car on the road. Normally, this was an easy task for me, but here the story was different. Avis denied knowing that the confirmed Johannesburg rental car requirements included air conditioning and an automatic shift. I had settled for a tiny, two-door vehicle with neither. Remembering to drive on the left side of the road, especially should an emergency occur, only increased my anxiety.

'Where can I find Gonubie Caravan Park?' I inquired. 'Go left,' one man said. Another yelled, 'no, no, start out by turning right.' This was before GPS navigation systems came in cars or smartphones, so I had little to guide me besides a general map, receiving directions from passersby, and my intuition.

Conflicting guidance often results when asking for directions. Locals may know locations in relation to someone's house, or maybe not at all if the site is where they have never visited. While liquor had helped these guides form an opinion on how to direct me, my weariness and my inability to follow their thick (to my American ears) South African accents, presented a challenge.

Then one helpful man came over to where I sat, apart from the others, explaining the directions more slowly. Language is often the traveller's challenge.

It was then that I realized why I had misunderstood the storm-jacketed, fuel attendant when he told me how to find the caravan park. I thought he had told me to turn just past the spa. No. He directed me to turn at the SPAR, the name given to a chain of supermarkets. I had been looking everywhere for a spa, of course, to no avail. Missing 'r's' can cause a lot of communication problems around the world.

While I had been searching for this elusive spa, the gale had intensified. I could no longer drive even a few feet. At the end of a street, with the sea on the other side of a low wall, I had pulled into a large unattended parking lot to wait out the storm. I changed from my driving clothes into my night dress tripling as a bathing suit coverup, and climbed into the car's backseat. Wiggling into my silk sleeping bag and wrapping the poncho over me, I planned to wait out the storm, praying not to be swept into the Indian Ocean a few feet away.

Parking lot sleeping in any country is not advisable — certainly not in South Africa, most would have told me — but I had little choice. Driving had become impossible as the storm raged. I could not see a sheep's body ahead of the car. I settled down to wait for the rain to subside.

My eyes closed only to hear a series of loud bangs. I yelled, sat up and screamed, 'No! NO! Get out, get out!!'

Was I being attacked in the middle of this storm when no one with any sense would be outside in it? Were robbers that desperate? Were wild animals nearby?

I peeked out the windows. I could see no one. The winds rocked the car side to side. Pelting rains were deafening on the car's roof and hood.

My heart was in my mouth. Terrified didn't begin to describe my emotional state.

Maybe something with enormous force had blown against the car. A coconut? A dead palm frond? I was not getting out to check. As soon as I could see ahead 4 feet, I started the engine and routed it up the incline, out of the parking lot.

Once more, I drove through the resort town, searching for the caravan park, touted as a great beachside location. Hotels and B&Bs looked either out of business or closed for the night. Not a single person, light or sign of life could be seen. If I could, I'd be staying under the covers, too.

Limited choices included heading toward the next town, but the storm forces would likely return, and then I'd be stuck again. The third time I passed Radillo's Pub and Pool, I chanced it.

Minutes later, given the bar customers' instructions, my weariness and the storm, I decided that these characters, drunk as they might be, were no more or less harmful than many I'd seen gathered at a redneck bar somewhere in the US. Through the mud, I slogged back to the car, pulled out a few rand and returned to have a glass of red wine poured from a box behind a wooden cabinet.

The rowdies left me to the bartender and the helpful man. Soon I was eating my first *biltong* (a South African form of soft jerky), trying to understand the English these two spoke. Within a few minutes they shared their fears about life in South Africa when Mandela died. Both wanted to leave the country if they could find a way. The helpful man told of a friend who had found a woman on the Internet who was taking him to the US.

Gusts and blowing wind subsided. Bar closing time arrived. The bartender assured me that I could follow him, and he would take me to the caravan park. The helpful man was returning to his side of town.

Only as I followed the bartender onto the highway, seeing his car swerve, did I realize how drunk he was. The night promised to be even longer.

Within a kilometre or so, he turned into the same fuel station I had visited previously. Five minutes later we were on our way, me following a respectable distance should he drive off the road.

We turned left, then right. I thanked the rain gods it was clear enough that I could see to drive. Suddenly, he pulled to the left, got out and came back to my car. Sheepishly he said, 'Sorry, I took a wrong turn.' Great, I thought. Just what I needed ... more lost time and insecurity. Could this guy be trusted?

Smiling sweetly and as confidently as I could muster, I replied with the well-worn phrase, 'No problem.' On we drove. I thought of all I had read, learned and taught about leadership and followership — yet here I was, following a drunk-driving bartender down the road in an unfamiliar part of the world! How brilliant was that?

Suddenly, to my left, I saw the Gonubie Caravan Park portal, hidden among heavy and leafy trees. I jerked the wheel in that direction. I glided past a couple of caravans, headed into a vacant campsite, and turned off my lights and engine. Confirming the doors were locked, I curled into the back seat for the second time that night.

I could hear car tyres spinning in the distance, the sound vehicles make when they are stuck in the mud. The bartender probably took another wrong turn.

I drifted off to sleep.

All Aboard

DIMITY POWELL

We were old-time travel hacks, my sister and I — seasoned professionals able to withstand any travel tribulation with just three pairs of socks and the budget of a nine-year-old. At least, that was our belief after close to nine months of backpacking around Europe and the Middle East.

We'd been resting and recouping in the multi-hued metropolis of London for much of the winter, harbouring a lingering regret; we had not *done everything*. 'Everything' was Portugal.

We arranged time off, dragged our dusty backpacks out from under the bed and dug out our trusty hiking socks — just two pairs this time; it was, after all, only one country.

'But why?' incredulous work colleagues bemoaned on hearing that we aimed to survive, divide and conquer this salt-cod-scented strip of the Iberian Peninsula, on just 25 pounds a day.

'Because we can,' we argued, reminding ourselves that we indeed had.

Our European adventures had involved repeated repasts of rollmops for breakfast in Bergen, sharing steam baths with semi-naked strangers in Münster, crossing the Austrian Alps with the agility and determination of the Von Trapps, and surviving teeming clouds of summer-time tourists in Venice.

Stewing in a 40-degree Athenian soup of diesel fumes and sweaty armpits was no different to enduring a typical South Australian summer, and the incessant clot of pension spruikers choking Aegean ports was just another annoyance we'd learnt to ignore, like the stink of our unwashed socks.

Bombings at the Gates of Damascus were an everyday occurrence we'd come to accept. Enduring the shits and spits in Cairo took a bit more intestinal fortitude. Rolling down an embankment in a bus, at night, and landing just metres from a railway track in the middle of Turkish nowhere was a disturbing re-enactment of the train wreck scene from *The Fugitive* and a means test of our mental and physical mettle. Nothing about *that* particular incident was more unnerving however, than the reverse-charges call home to the parents explaining how we'd survived a dramatic bus crash. They seemed spectacularly unimpressed with our descriptions of the Black Sea town of Ünye, where we convalesced.

We'd returned to England the colour of mallee roots and scrawnier than dogs on diets of seawater, bone weary but triumphant, ever-so-slightly traumatized but quietly impressed with ourselves. Risk and danger morph easily into adventure when you don't have enough currency to make any other choice. We'd survived biting cold and virulent heat, cultural indifference and gastric disturbances comparable to small earthquakes. How hard could it be to explore one more relatively civilized country? The only way to find out was to go.

Portugal was all we'd hoped for: terracotta-coloured beaches, cauldrons of *bacalhau* (dried and salted cod) washed down with cheap rosé, achingly beautiful ceramic work adorning every street corner. If our rambles were more prosaic than our previous expeditions, it was because the 'been there, done that' mentality was difficult to dislodge. We felt we had little more to prove. Or so we thought.

Forgoing the rugged allure of Portugal's mountainous, wolf-inhabited national parks, we decided that a brief visit to Porto would be sufficient homage to its northern regions.

Tucked away at the mouth of the Douro River, Porto was an overnight train trip from Portimão with a change of trains in the country's capital at Estação do Oriente. A doddle, we thought, having withstood the pickpockets and occasional carriage hijackings of central Europe. Maintaining a veneer of aloof assuredness was our tried-and-tested technique.

The night train to Lisbon was erringly empty. A handful of individuals stared blankly at reflections of themselves in windows darkened by severe carriage lighting. We chose a sparsely populated carriage with rows of seats facing both directions. Settling in, we could almost smell the rich aromas of coffee and creamy *bola de Berlim* (Portuguese doughnuts) breakfast that awaited us the next morning.

Then we noticed them, one Caucasian, the other a dark-skinned Brazilian. Both with a malignant demeanour that set our nerves dancing. As the train pulled out of Portimão, the pair settled into a double seat half a dozen rows in front of ours. Their back-facing seats afforded them an uninterrupted view of us. Neither my sister nor I uttered a sound, furtively glancing their way now and then, anxious to gauge their intent, scared to make eye contact. Everything felt wrong.

They shared conspiratorial whispers, dark eyes glued upon us. Clots of incomprehensible Portuguese roiled like toxic vapours through the carriage, poisoning our sense of wellbeing.

Stay aloof. Look assured. Fear can be smelt. I kept repeating this mantra to myself despite mounting apprehension.

'They're going to rob us,' whispered my sister. Her absolute conviction that they meant us harm both unnerved and infuriated me. *Were they? How dare they? What had we done to elicit this fate? How could we avoid it?* My thoughts had become as erratic as my breathing.

I stole a glance around our near-empty carriage. We decided to haul our packs into the adjoining, better populated carriage. They followed, seating themselves a few rows away. The irrational assumption that we'd become their prey fuelled fear and an urge to flee, but we had nowhere to run. The train continued to rock its way through blackened landscapes, indifferent to the drama unfolding within its innards.

For a long while, they continued to stare, openly ominous. We waited, rigid with dread and foreboding like antelopes ready to bolt. Silence smothered the carriage like a mortician's shroud. Around midnight, the train slid into Estação do Oriente.

Passengers dispersed into the dark, becoming part of the night as we made our way to the ticket counter. Our connecting train was still half an hour away. We had no choice but to wait. Rounding a corner, we spotted them. It took me a moment to process their absence of luggage, not even a daypack.

We retreated to the perceived sanctuary of the ticket counter, reasoning the closer we were to another human being, the safer we would be. My sister shivered behind her backpack, edgy and spent. This was wrong. I loathed feeling so vulnerable and helpless. I wanted this to end.

Leaving my pack with her, I strode out of the waiting area onto the open platform charged with uncertain determination. Searching. Angry. Challenging. *How dare they?* This surge of fearlessness surprised me because I had no clear plan of how to enforce my point against two menacing males twice my size.

'Come back!' hissed my sister.

Ignoring her, I found them languishing in the shadows at the end of the platform, patiently waiting for the train to arrive. Their assured calm enraged me. I faced them with the stance of a gunslinger at high noon. As they glanced casually my way, a new thought jolted my resolve: *What if we were wrong? What if they were just two lads traversing the countryside with no other agenda other than spending some quality time together?* It sounded implausible even to me but what if fear had clouded my judgment? I faulted in the dingy light but hoped my weak non-verbal confrontation had shown them this was one antelope that would not be pulled easily asunder.

I returned to my sister and watched a willowy young man push his bicycle to a vacant seat. Pale faced under the pasty lighting, his eyes glazed by the tediousness of long-distance travel, he wore glasses and an expression of benign reliability. We immediately edged closer, venturing a greeting in broken Portuguese. He responded in German, a language we both had more knowledge of, and in hushed, rushed tones we described our concerns and asked to remain by his side until our train arrived.

The fact that he was ill-built to single-handedly fight off two would-be aggressors or could have been a psychopath himself was quickly dismissed. We needed to feel safe. He was our only option, an option that promised fewer dire consequences than any others.

Finally, the train rattled in and we clambered aboard. We found the same open-seating arrangement, the same brutal lighting, and the same sinister presence, but with one major difference: the carriages were humming with the howling of dozens of drunken national service soldiers, celebrating god knows what. They guffawed and cock-a-doodle-dooed up and down the carriage, some slumped into their seats, while others took advantage of the overhead luggage racks to sleep off their inebriety. None of them paid us the slightest attention. We pushed into the rowdiest knot of them, smiling weakly for the first time in hours, torrential relief flooding our every nerve. Deciding we were finally safe, we dozed, our stalkers forgotten, lost in the throng of black military uniforms, until we pulled into Campanhã Railway Station in Porto.

As an egg-custard dawn oozed across the Douro River, we farewelled bicycle man and headed for the nearest *pastelaria* (pastry shop), eager to find accommodation and purge ourselves of last night's nightmare. It was time to change our socks and fortify frazzled nerves with a few ports. After all, when in Rome ...

A Short Walk on the Streets of Duhok

NATASHA SEYMOUR

It started with a conversation in Istanbul. It was nearly the end of the day, and Ciaran and I were visiting the city's Kadïkoy district, drinking çay (Turkish tea) by the skirt of the Bosphorus Strait. The original plan was to travel north along the Black Sea coast towards Georgia, but a week in Istanbul had spurred into me a curiosity about Middle Eastern culture and conjured up an appetite for adventure that went beyond our plan to stay on the tourist trail. We re-routed, deciding to travel south-east towards the Turkish city of Mardin, where ancient Mesopotamian land extends from Turkey into Syria and Iraq. From our base in Mardin, we would make our journey to the city of Duhok, in the Kurdistan Region of Iraq.

The morning we left Mardin for Duhok, we had eggs for breakfast. We were staying with a young French expatriate named Marie and another French backpacker named

Romain, who would also be travelling to Iraq that day, although not with us. Ciaran and I had plans to take a bus to Duhok, while Romain was committed to a hitchhiking streak that had seen him through Italy, Greece, Turkey and Iran. That morning we talked over a fresh batch of coffee and prepared to face the staunch heat of the day.

Iraqi Kurdistan is a semi-autonomous region in northern Iraq. It has been a parliamentary democracy since 1992, when Kurdish rebels achieved de-facto independence from the Iraqi government. Economic embargoes and disagreements over land and oil dragged out the conflict until an official ceasefire agreement was made in 1998 with the help of US intervention. Now, the Kurdistan Regional Government (KRG) and the Kurdish military, the *Peshmerga*, are more or less independent from the rest of Iraq, although this tenuous relationship is always changing. This means that for tourists, Iraqi Kurdistan is a relatively safe and dynamic place to travel, and I was, like so many people, enthralled by this history.

The bus to Duhok left Mardin at 12:00 p.m. from the main *otogar* (bus terminal), where there are a handful of tourism companies running direct routes to the capital city of Erbil, stopping in Duhok. The bus was full, but we were the only foreigners in a sea of Iraqi and Turkish men and women who regularly commute back and forth to see family or for work. The bus makes a short stop at Cizre, and then at Silopi, which is the last city before the border crossing, and closely hugs the Syrian border for most of the journey.

The drive was surreal; the land was arid and sprawling, and the border was marked by barbed wire fencing and military outposts. In the distance, we could see the shells of houses fallen into piles of rubble, baking in the midday sun. Our vehicle crossed the Ibrahim Khalil border with little fuss. We were instructed to line up to show our passports and then taken to the customs office to have them stamped. They asked us no questions on either side and only took a photo and a thumbprint for their records.

Once on the other side, we stopped at the city of Zakho, where we were able to buy snacks with Turkish *lira* and receive Iraqi *dinar* as change. Closer to Duhok, our bus passed through a long range of sloping, dog-toothed mountains that flank the banks of the Tigris River, which runs from eastern Turkey all the way into Baghdad, where it joins the Persian Gulf.

When we arrived in Duhok, it was late afternoon and we had been travelling all day. We took our packs from the belly of the bus and hailed a taxi that took us into the central bazaar. In Duhok's main square, there was a lot to take in. My thoughts, which were, at that moment, on the task of crossing the road, were choked by the thick smell of spices, the sound of cars honking and the colourful fabrics of the bazaar. In a daze, we wove through the chaos, walking in the direction of a guesthouse we had read about online that was supposedly cheap. We were greeted by the owner of a shop selling tech supplies, who told us that our 'backpackers' house was out of business and pointed us in the direction of another hotel.

Ciaran bargained with the hotel owner for a cheap room. The man wrote '20' on a piece of paper, meaning 20,000 dinar. Ciaran typed '10' into his phone and held it up, and there was a pause where I wondered if it was offensive to ask for such a low price. But the man just smiled agreeably and nodded, and we were left alone in a small room with a window that gave us a view of the street, which was now hazy in the softer light.

We sent a quick message to Romain, who wouldn't turn up until very late that night, and left the hotel in search of food. It was the beginning of summer, and the weather, which was unbearably hot during the day, was only marginally cooler after sunset. Despite the heat, men and women alike were in heavy clothing. Many of the women wore a pinned headdress, called a *hijab*, over their hair and neck, and younger men were dressed in modern clothing: long jeans and sleeved shirts. The older men wore traditional Kurdish dress, which consists of wide beige trousers, a matching jacket and a long gown, tied together with a large sash around the waist — the modern and the traditional, coexisting.

In the coolness of the indoor bazaar, we found a small shop selling fresh rolls filled with chicken and grilled vegetables. Inside the shop we watched attentively as groups of men talked with one another while they waited, and I felt slightly out of place as the only female in the crowd. This feeling would only be exacerbated later that week as it became apparent that women were often confined to separate quarters of public society while the men worked and socialized freely.

As a western woman, many of the rules that applied to Muslim women did not apply to me. However, my encounters with men were often complicated by these customs, and more than once I went to shake the hand of a new acquaintance only to be met with embarrassment or even, at times, laughter. The next morning, I came across a group of women of different ages, gathered on the cold tiles of a women's public bathroom. They looked up at me as I came in, and I had the feeling of being estranged from both the women in this room and the men out in the world.

After dinner that night, we walked through the market, which was doused in the darkness of a brief power outage and made our way back towards the hotel. Once again, I was acutely aware of the women in the crowd — almost invisible amongst the men who filled out the narrow spaces — and I felt tempted to break off from the safety of my group to give them a small sign of my kinship with them: a nod of the head, a small smile, or utterance of the words '*As-salamu alaikum*', which means 'peace be with you' in Arabic. But I was afraid of the unspoken divide between us; me, a western woman with the privilege to travel where I pleased, to do what I felt like in the moment, and them, women with unbreakable ties to their culture, to their families and to the honour of their fathers and husbands.

As we wandered, I glanced behind us and saw the mountains rising up into the sky, claimed by the Kurdish flag — three bands of red, white and green, and a golden sun in its center, a symbol of renaissance, revival, and a new beginning.

A Home-grown Tourist

NATASHA GARRETT

'Don't speak English when we are in the taxi,' I remind my son. 'Actually, don't speak at all.'

'Why?'

'Because I don't want the taxi driver to think we are tourists.'

We have a version of this conversation every time we visit Ohrid, a small town in my home country of Macedonia. On the surface, it is a money-saving strategy; I have a feeling that if the taxi driver thinks we are tourists, he would charge us more, or at least expect a more generous tip. But taxi drivers everywhere are savvy, and they quickly figure out that I am not from Ohrid — a local would likely walk or ride a bike, not hail a taxi like a total outsider.

'*Od Skopje si?*' asks the taxi driver. 'Are you from Skopje?'

My accent betrays me. When speaking Macedonian, I can't hide the fact that indeed I am from Skopje, the capital of Macedonia. I was born in Skopje and lived there until I was eighteen years old when I left to go to college in the United States. However, my parents moved from Skopje to Ohrid a decade ago, and I consider the picturesque, touristy lakeside town my Macedonian home. And touristy it is, especially in the summer when it fills up with droves of teenagers, groups of fanny-packed Central Europeans wearing sun visors, families from neighbouring Balkan countries and quite a few people who live abroad and spend their vacation with their families here. People like me.

Declared a World Heritage Site by UNESCO, this 'pearl of the Balkans', as it is often called, Ohrid charms with its medieval architecture, cultural richness and natural beauty. It sits on the shores of Lake Ohrid, one of the deepest and oldest lakes in Europe. It is estimated that the lake originated five million years ago, unusual for a lake. Only Lake Baikal in Russia and Lake Tanganyika in eastern Africa share a similarly long history.

If you walk up the cobblestone streets in the old part of town, you will get to St Clement Church, the home of the oldest university in the Balkans. A short walk up the hill, and you will reach Samuil's Fortress and be rewarded with great views of the town below, the blue expanse of the lake extending to neighboring Albania, and the wreath of mountains buttressing the shores and offering a perfect jump-off point for the numerous paragliders dotting the sky. The shore is punctuated by a variety of beaches, from smaller and quieter ones closer to town, where local retirees meet early in the morning for sunbathing and local gossip, to busier ones, populated by many young bodies, with open-air bars and the relentless thump of electronic music pulsing in the air. In the evenings, you can attend one of the many performances offered during the Ohrid Summer Festival, go out for a dinner of local *plashica* (fish and white wine), or take a walk on the promenade to the port and through the Old Bazaar, a mandatory ice-cream cone in hand. Tourist perfection.

The thing is, I don't want to be a tourist. I'm afraid of being a tourist. It is often a challenge for me, as it is for many immigrants nowadays, to feel at home in my adopted country. Not because it is not a welcoming place, though sometimes it can be, but because I will always be perceived as someone not from the States. My English is still slightly accented, my Christmas is in January, my family lives thousands of miles away. I find respite from my state of otherness when I come home to Macedonia. I have feared becoming a foreigner in my own homeland.

My visits have shortened, from four months a year when I was a student to three weeks in the summer, a very long vacation by US standards and laughably short for Macedonians. When in Ohrid, I fear losing touch with the everyday rhythm of life back in the US — I am, after all, on vacation, and in my leisurely days of sleeping in, enjoying family meals, swimming, sipping *Zlaten Dab* beer on our balcony or hiking the hills above the town, I am spared the stress of ordinary life, whether it is inefficient bureaucracy, annoying neighbours or occasional political instability. I have feared that not always knowing about a new popular band or a TV show or a trendy restaurant will further push me towards the territory of being just a tourist among the other tourists enjoying a portion of the summer in Ohrid.

My husband, a fair-skinned, blonde, bearded American in bright shirts, looks like a legitimate tourist, and by extension, makes me stick out — a local girl who married a foreigner. But having him and our son with me when going home eases my fear of 'not belonging', of perhaps overthinking it all. In their eyes, I fit in perfectly. They get to see me and my family in our natural habitat, and whatever habits I have that look quirky in the States, make perfect sense here.

Our son is especially curious about the place. During his first visit, when he was seven years old, he soberly pronounced, 'It is great here, but we need more public access wi-fi and more public toilets.' He loves the places that connect him further with my side of the family. I give him the real insider tour. 'This is where your grandma attended high school. This is the old cinema building. Here is the emergency room, also known as "malaria clinic". My grandma and I used to buy cherries from this market and sit by the lake and eat them.' He takes it all in. When he goes hiking with my Dad, he looks for the walking sticks they hid in the bushes the previous summer. To his amazement, they are still there. This boy, born on a different continent and with an imperfect knowledge of the Macedonian language, knows that Ohrid is a part of him and his family history. He is not afraid of claiming more than one place as his own, and neither should I.

'I was born in Skopje,' I admit to the taxi driver. 'But we live here now.'

I don't go into details, but I don't think I am inaccurate. We are here now, living in the moment, soaking in the feeling, as short-lived as it may be, that we are truly at home.

The Echo of Solitude

STEFANIE RÖFKE

Thick fog hung over the fields and meadows as I set out in the early morning hours to venture further north on the Pennine Way. Cows and sheep watched me with interest as I marched right through their herds. I was an unusual site in this lonely landscape with my brimming rucksack and the clacking of my walking sticks. Soon afterwards, I had disappeared from their world, and they lowered their heads again to graze the dew-damp grass that surrounded them like a fluffy carpet.

It didn't take long before the silhouette of an enormous hill emerged before me through the veil of fog.

Despite days of hauling myself up and down the terrain, my body had yet to adapt to the steep inclines. I slowly climbed up to the summit, panting. And then I stood there again, completely alone on the backbone of the Pennines. The hills were covered in a scratchy blanket of heather, a vast expanse of purple that stretched out to the horizon. Now and again the landscape changed to the copper of grass plateaus, then to the deep green of grassy meadows. A sandy path snaked its way through the high and lonely moors.

This high up I was unlikely to come across any human company. In such solitude, the only voice to be heard was the echo of my own. Being alone for hours and days felt strange to me. I'd always been surrounded by people somehow, or at least it would have been easy for me to contact them. Out here, I didn't have a network connection. My smartphone wasn't a high-performance computer that connected me to the world any more. Instead, it was just something that I could use as a camera. And at the time, I didn't realize I took pictures of a landscape whose real beauty was more elusive than a photo could capture.

The fact that I couldn't reach anyone also meant that nobody could reach me either. The feeling of relief, that things would just have to wait until I got home, was something I hadn't known before. Slowly, the sense of being far away from everyday life began to manifest itself. For a while now, my thoughts hadn't been about the tasks that I hadn't done or what I was missing on the computer, television or radio. It would have seemed completely absurd to me to put headphones on and drown out the noises around me with an MP3 player. I wished to merge with my surroundings and have the landscape accept me.

Still, I *did* hear a kind of music out there. The rustling of my rucksack, my shoes scuffing along the ground, the song of the sky larks and the clucking of the moorhens created a soundtrack that followed my journey as if it had been written just for me. In these hours I was in complete harmony with the present. My thoughts were unfocused and free. I didn't think about anything in particular. Instead, in silence, I listened to how the world around me began to speak. It told me of the dark woods that once covered the barren highland areas of the Pennines and of the wild wolves that roamed there. I discovered tribal conflicts, and Celtic myths, stone fortresses, and kingdoms that have now disappeared. I was in a land of ancient history that lay hidden beneath my feet. This region didn't seem to belong to anyone apart from the sheep, whose black heads peeped out of the bushes here and there.

Completely in awe, I lost sight of the path. My feet, which before had been stirring up dust on the dry ground, were now stuck in a bog. The heather had disappeared and given way to another type of vegetation. Carefully, I made a path for myself through reed grass, which was up to my hips, and through vibrant peat moss.

I couldn't find a sure footing anywhere. As soon as I put one of my feet down, the ground gave way. I sank down to my knees in warm mud. Crippling fear crawled through my veins, and I knew that the only person whom I could rely on right now was me.

I saved myself by climbing onto a small patch of grass and started thinking.

I had spent the last night amongst the turmoil of a busy camp site. The wind had tugged at the tent like a hungry harpy. Sleep was out of the question. The two plastic bottles, which I had previously filled with hot water to keep me warm, had cooled after only 10 minutes. I froze terribly in my thin sleeping bag, which was unsuitable for the cool nights of late summer. Now, my lack of sleep was having an unfavourable impact on my sense of direction. At least the fog had cleared, but gloomy clouds were beginning to darken the sky. Little droplets of water fell on my face and mixed with the stream of salty tears that ran over my cheeks.

A spongy carpet lay before me, under which unknown chasms were lurking. My head filled with gruesome stories about the insatiable moor that dragged everything that tried to cross it down into its depths. I realized that, as a city kid who had been spoiled and surrounded by concrete, I had no idea how I should behave in this kind of terrain other than to stand still, sobbing and hoping help would come.

Against this scary backdrop, breathing became difficult. The Pennine Way had completely disappeared under a sea of black mud. Next to me, the gnawed skeleton of a bird poked out of the marshy ground. I imagined how, next spring, my remains would be found by passing hikers alongside it. 'This is what happens when city folk come to the Pennine Way!' they'd say, shaking their heads dispassionately and then carrying on their way.

If only someone were here to speak encouraging words to me. With a companion, everything would be more bearable.

But then I took a deep breath and reminded myself that this exact thing was my challenge. I had wanted to master this alone, in spite of my fears, and that meant grabbing myself by my collar and pulling myself out of this mess.

I wiped away my tears with the dirt-encrusted sleeve of my jacket. Then, I divided the mud into smaller sections in my mind and crossed it, going from one tiny patch of grass to the next, teetering like a clumsy stork. After many hours, I felt solid ground beneath my feet. I drew in a breath and looked back.

A squeaky shout of relief came from my throat. Shortly afterwards, it rose to a battle cry. I was completely alone on this merciless trail that demanded so much of me. For the first time in my life, I realized what it meant to be thrown back on my own abilities. But most importantly, I understood that I wasn't really alone. I was with the best companion there was — me.

My First Time Flying Alone

LORENZO GAERTNER

We came to a sign that said, 'Passengers Only Beyond This Point', so I hugged my parents tightly and promised to text them regular updates. Then I grabbed my suitcases and headed for the departure hall, where a woman in uniform watched me approach from behind her desk. I was nervous. She could tell.

'Hiya, luv. Got yeh boardin' pass?' she said, sounding bored.

'Hiya,' I said, mimicking her Leeds accent. I was trying to remember what people had told me about talking to airport staff — keep it snappy, don't try to be clever, don't lose your temper — and, not hearing what she had said, I handed her my passport.

'Yeh boardin' pass, luv,' she repeated.

'Oh right, sorry,' I said, fumbling about in my pockets. As

a kid I used to think that getting on a plane seemed like the most stressful thing in the world. I never knew why, just that when we were at the airport my parents never seemed relaxed and we weren't really allowed to play. There were no e-tickets then, so Mum kept all our passports and documents in a fat plastic wallet which she clutched as though she were holding the manuscript of a new Harry Potter book. I was amazed when I found out that you actually only need one piece of paper to board a flight now. I fished that piece of paper out of my pocket and handed it to the woman.

'Where y'off teh?' she asked, only half looking up at me.

'Dakar, Senegal,' I said.

'What's the purpose o' yer trip?'

'I'm visiting relatives there.'

'Ow long yeh goin' for?'

'Three months.'

She raised her eyebrows. 'Bit of a long visit, that.'

I wasn't sure if that was supposed to be a question, so I nodded and fake-laughed a bit and muttered something vague like, 'Yeah, well, you know how it is.' Then she held my boarding pass under her scanner and something on her computer monitor flashed green.

''Ave a good journey, luv.'

'Thanks.'

My sister and I used to play games where we'd pretend to be grown-ups with jobs to go to and kids to look after and housework to catch up on. Our bedrooms would become miniature supermarkets replete with toy food, which we'd pay for with old library cards that we pretended were credit cards. I still remember the surreal feeling of paying with a real credit card in a real shop for the first time, and how grown-up it made me feel. That feeling hit me again now as I checked in for my first flight. It was just like playing those old games, only not in a sheltered, imaginary world where I made the rules but a harsh, confusing world where somebody else did, a world I was slowly learning to navigate. I looked back to where my parents were still standing, waving to them as one would wave before boarding a spaceship to Mars. Then I turned the corner, out of their sight and into the cold, unwelcoming arms of British customs.

* * *

I put my bag on the conveyor belt like everybody else, but the metal detector beeped when I walked through it, and a short, grumpy officer with foul breath motioned me to the side while the other passengers went ahead. I thought I was going to end up like the people on *Banged Up Abroad*, the TV show where they re-enact stories of people being thrown in prison for trying to sneak drugs through airport security. I'm sure almost every episode begins with the main character being taken away by customs officials.

The officer told me to take off my shoes and put my hands on the wall in front of me. Then he patted me down — *all* of me — and gave me a once-over with his handheld metal detector. I knew I wasn't carrying anything illegal, and yet I was terrified of this man and his bleeping, crackling little machine. After a brief search he grunted something that I took to mean 'alright, fuck off' and waved me away. I put my shoes back on and headed for the gate feeling rattled and lonely. My parents had barely made it to the carpark, but already it felt like they were a million miles away.

There were no direct flights from Leeds to Dakar, so I had to take a short flight to Brussels and get a connecting flight from there. I was hoping that the security staff in Brussels would be nicer than the ones in Leeds. They were, but when I got to the gate to get my connecting flight and found a queue of people already waiting there, something else occurred to me, something subtle and yet far more profound than being groped by the unfriendly customs officer back in Yorkshire. I realized that, for the first time in my life, I was the only white person in the room.

✳ ✳ ✳

As naïve as it may sound, the thought that I might ever stand out for being white had genuinely never occurred to me. I was born in South Africa, but in all our visits back there after moving to the UK, my brother and sister and I barely met anyone who wasn't one of our friends or family — and who wasn't white. The only black people we ever got to know there were the two whom my grandparents employed to look after the house. And the small town in northern England where I grew up wasn't exactly what you'd call cosmopolitan, either. Until going to Senegal, pretty much everybody I'd ever met had been white.

I was grateful to be where I was, to be offered a new perspective. Having lived in the UK, I was from a different country, a different continent than all my friends, but I'd never known how it felt to look like an outsider, too. And I was one of the lucky ones. In Senegal, I would be treated like royalty because of the colour of my skin. How unwelcoming it must be for the people who come to the UK and are treated as welfare leeches or terrorists.

I stood for a long while, feeling conspicuous. A young woman appeared to my right and seemed to be looking straight at me. I kept my head down, hoping she would go away.

'Vous-êtes dernier?' she asked, making me jump.

'Sorry?' I muttered back.

'Vous-êtes dernier?'

I knew enough French to understand what she was saying but couldn't make sense of the words. My head was too full. I looked at her blankly. She asked again, this time pointing to the queue for the gate that seemed to end with me. My brain finally kicked in: dernier – last! She's asking if I'm last in the queue.

'Ah, oui!' I said.

'Merci,' she said. She dropped her bags and stood in line

behind me with her arms crossed, gazing absently around the room. She didn't seem to give a shit that I was white.

The plane was restless and noisy. As it was taking off, one of the panels from the overhead storage came loose and crashed into the aisle in front of me, and I saw some of the other passengers making the sign of the cross and clasping their hands in prayer. Others simply shrieked. But then it was replaced, dinner was served, and then they dimmed the lights and everything went still. Exhausted, I put on my headphones and drifted off to sleep and was woken some hours later by a voice coming over the PA system: 'Ladies and gentlemen, we are now beginning our descent into Dakar ...' I leaned over to look out the window. It was almost pitch-dark outside but for the lights of the city and the impressive new African Renaissance Monument. We flew over the airport and out to sea before making a wide, graceful, 270-degree turn which suspended us momentarily over the twinkling lights of a few scattered ships dotting the dark waters below. Then we landed, and like that my first solo journey was over. I couldn't wait to catch up with my relatives and begin exploring the city, and I stepped out into the heat and the noise and the unfamiliarity of Dakar feeling more grown-up than I'd ever felt before.

Overcoming Fear in Iran, One Breath at a Time

KERSTIN PILZ

I am holding onto the metal side panel of the fire-engine red *tuk-tuk* until my knuckles go white. With my other hand I am desperately trying to keep myself covered, clutching the ends of my white headscarf in a tight fist with the ends of my black manteau.

We are hurtling over potholes, at full speed, on the wrong side of the road, chasing the sunset on Hormuz Island, in the south of Iran.

Yusuf, our twenty-something driver with a cool hipster hair-do and red soccer shirt, drives his *tuk-tuk* like a modern beast of burden through the rocky interior of the island.

I can't remember the last time I have felt this scared. The Persian Gulf flashes into view, a pearl-coloured carpet of stillness, before it disappears again as we fly around another bend. I feel the wheels momentarily leave the road and let out a high-pitched scream.

Yusuf turns around with a surprised smile. 'You okay?' No, I am definitely not okay. I am scared to death of ending up down the ravine that opens beside us. My bones feel rattled and I am forever strangling myself as my headscarf becomes entangled with the straps of my camera. Not to speak of the permanent bad-hair day a veil gives you.

I am not sure that Yusuf would understand any of my fears and frustrations, and besides, we share less than a handful of words. 'Yes,' I say, 'I am okay.' I smile back at him in the side mirror. He motions me to adjust my scarf, then he opens the throttle and we're off again.

Just as I am making a mental list of the different worst-case scenarios for our high-speed sunset chase, the *tuktuk* begins to slow as we roll down a steep hill, until we come to a complete standstill.

The monumental landscape of the Mars-like, deserted, interior of Hormuz Island gradually comes into focus. The silence after our roaring ride is overwhelming.

Yusuf tries the throttle a few times, but his beast is dead. We've broken down amid barren clusters of rock that look like shavings of thick dark brown chocolate, sprinkled here and there with hues of white, pink, yellow and purple.

The worst-case scenario, it turns out, is missing the sunset over the Strait of Hormuz on our last evening in Iran.

Yusuf smiles and squats beside his vehicle to fix a previously botched wiring job.

I take a deep breath and remind myself that travel is all about being in the moment, trusting the flow.

This is just one of the many mindfulness challenges our month-long trip through Iran has offered. Our journey has taken us from the green lushness of the Caspian Sea, through deserts and the fabled cities of central Iran, all the way down to the Persian Gulf.

Every day delivered the unexpected. Iran has been a crash course in what Zen Buddhists call 'beginner's mind'. It refers to the practice of looking at the world without expectations, as if seeing everything for the first time. It helps to let go of stress, anxiety and fear. I was familiar with the theory. Iran challenged me to practise it.

I had stepped into Imam Khomeini International Airport one month earlier stressed, anxious and fearful of the unknown. My ears were ringing with alarmist headlines that declared Iran one of the world's most dangerous places. My stomach was in a knot with the fears of well-meaning friends and family. 'Things can flare up there at any moment,' I was told over and over. I didn't have the courage to tell my parents that I was going anyway.

At over 50, feeling this way seemed ridiculous. The last time I had felt this anxious about travel was when I'd left Germany on a one-way ticket to Jakarta, a fresh-faced, blond, 21-year old female solo traveller.

Getting ready for Iran was like preparing to survive in an alien land. Facebook and Airbnb, two platforms on which I run my business, are banned in Iran. Like everybody else, I downloaded a VPN (virtual private network). All throughout the flight I felt like a spy sneaking into the 'world's most dangerous country' with a dangerous piece of software in my pocket.

My partner and I are the only two white people to get off the flight from Doha in Qatar.

A tall man takes my passport, turns away and talks for the longest time in a loud voice to a uniformed man. I focus on my breath. There is nothing to worry about. I have read a dozen blogs about how to get your entrance visa on arrival for Iran. But I worry that we are not married. That I have brought the wrong passport photos. That a wet stain on my scarf may be seen as a public offence.

The latest headlines about Iran that flashed across my screen before I turned my devices off are on repeat in my head, like a broken record. I breathe in and out evenly. It calms me, until a man who looks like a character out of a pre-Revolution movie steps into my field of vision. I focus on his square glasses and the 1970s cut of his grey suit, as I keep breathing, in and out. His English is limited but very precise. 'Pay here. In Euro is okay. Now you wait.' Before we have a chance to wait, he's back. 'Your passport. Welcome to Iran.' He smiles and puts his right hand on his heart.

It took less than 45 minutes to enter Iran, faster than I have ever entered any country. Being a guest in this alien land was easy from the moment we arrived but finding our flow in a country that dances to a foreign rhythm remains a daily challenge in mindfulness.

Yusuf taps me on the shoulder. He has fixed the wires. We resume our journey at break-neck speed over a patch of unsealed road. We do the final stretch on foot, running down steep canyons and up rocky ravines. I watch with envy as his feet glide assuredly in worn-out plastic slippers over the uneven rocks that shimmer pink in the fading light.

I lose sight of him and call into the darkness as the boulders around me seem to move in a little closer. I find him sitting on a small ledge, below him the cliff falls away in a 20-metre drop.

In front of us the Strait of Hormuz, the world's current tinderbox of political conflict, extends peaceful and empty, veiled in a soft pink haze. There was no magical sunset tonight. We have missed nothing. Six tankers line the horizon, like toys in a bathtub. On a clear day you can probably just see the tip of the Arabian Peninsula. To our right a sheer cliff extends in shades of purple as far as the eye can see. At the bottom the sand shimmers in hues of charcoal under the gentle splashes of the Persian Gulf.

Yusuf is on his phone. I join him with trembling knees and give him the thumbs up. Until smartphones and emoticons, the 'thumbs up' was the Iranian equivalent of the middle finger. But I know Yusuf will understand my gesture as intended.

I am too scared to pull out my camera. It would take one wrong move for it to topple over the edge with me following behind. To watch the fading beauty of the Persian Gulf in front of me, I have to be totally in the moment, taking conscious, even breaths.

The fear of falling down the cliff is different from the fear I felt about coming to Iran. Both take me out of my comfort zone and both make me feel alive. Travel off the beaten track is a rare opportunity to experience the world through the lens of 'beginner's mind'.

When we get back to the *tuktuk*, Yusuf motions us to turn around. A full moon is rising over the mountains on the leeward side of the island. It's the perfect finale to our month in Iran, a country that has made us feel safe and welcome in so many different ways. From hugs by random strangers, to cups of cinnamon tea and conversations about Persian poetry with our hosts, to the home-cooked meals and many sincere *salams* (greetings meaning 'peace'), everybody has greeted us like the airport official on our first day. Welcome to Iran. *Khosh amadid.* I heard these words repeated so often, I will never forget my sprinkling of Farsi. I have never felt so welcome and safe in an alien land.

Childhood Grievances in Eastern Australia

RUTH JONES

I hadn't seen my brother in almost two years.

If I was a better person (and a better biographer), I'd be able to describe a tearful farewell before he departed for pastures unknown. Truthfully, I can't remember it. There are four years between us, him older, and several years of, if not bad blood, then not-so-good blood. I told people he went to Australia and they would asked, 'Will you visit?', and I would reply, 'But what about the spiders?'

It took two years for me and my parents to fly from the UK to Sydney to see him. After the 24-hour flight, he met me at the airport looking nothing like how I remembered him. His beard was longer and bushier, and he'd bulked up. I thought that if I hadn't known I was meeting him, I might not have recognized my own brother. He helped carry my suitcase to the taxi and seemed excited I was there. I described to him the boredom of the long flight with the casual familiarity of a well-established relationship. In the back of the car, my eyes roamed for the spiders I still worried were skulking out of sight, feeling relieved when none appeared. I thought I may have let my imagination get the better of me, that the streets of urban Sydney weren't covered in roiling masses of malevolent arachnids, and perhaps my sibling bond was stronger than I had realized.

When people asked about my brother, I used to qualify it with 'we don't get on very well.' I didn't have his phone number. He didn't know the names of my friends. 'We're not close,' I would say. I got sporadic updates from my parents as to what he was doing in Australia. He's leaving the Sunshine Coast for Melbourne. Spending a few days at Byron Bay. Saw a spider the size of a man's head in a toilet at Coffs Harbour. We're thinking of visiting him next March, would you like to come?

My fingernails left reddened semi circles in my palms, but I agreed to go anyway. I pictured myself never going to the bathroom, too scared of what crept hidden through the pipes. I envisioned seeing my brother for the first time in two years and having nothing to say to him. I predicted leaving with the already fragile pieces of our relationship ground down into a fine dust.

I never used to be scared of spiders. One very clear memory prevails of me and my brother watching a chunky one lumber down the pavement, its long, hairy legs not quite strong enough for its body. 'I don't get it,' I'd said. 'What's so terrifying?' I must have been about five, me and him still in that stage of natural sibling friendship where we traded jabs and watched the movie *Congo* because he knew I was frightened of the gorillas.

On that first day in Sydney, I wore too-warm leggings and the built-up tension of months of worrying. My brother seemed surprised that I wanted to see the Sydney Opera House and the Harbour Bridge. He said you got used to it, living in Sydney, and he had other things to show me. The Royal Botanical Gardens bloomed with the contradiction of the exotic and the familiar, and he let me spend far too long trying to entice the cockatoos to come closer. When the sun crept towards noon, he bought me a lemonade and described how his day-to-day routine hadn't changed much. We sat almost silently over lunch. *It's fine*, I thought. *It's normal that we haven't got much to say.* At his flat he told me about the cockroaches and the bats, and I perched on the edge of his sofa watching the shadowy nooks between his furniture, unable to fully relax with the threat of spiders always lurking in the corner of my mind. In the botanical gardens he led me over to a tree absolutely dripping in spiders, their webs forming a lacy covering like a wrapped bouquet. I had been wearing mirrored aviator sunglasses, which I hoped masked my fear as cool disinterest.

For several childhood years Australia had been my number one travel destination, before I learnt that the deep ancestral part of my brain that feared multitudes of inky black legs wasn't as quiet as I thought it was. It was very silly to skip a childhood dream because I was worried about spiders. It was also stupid to miss out on a foreign adventure because I felt I had nothing to say to my brother.

Before I left, I watched TV shows set at zoos and purposely didn't change the channel when the insect house came on. When I lay awake at night, I pictured the insects sneaking through wine bars, biding their time under hotel sheets. In other moments, I brainstormed possible conversation topics for my brother. *Remember ages four to ten?*

We'd been close as children. Then less close. Then drifted far enough apart that you'd hardly remember we were close to begin with. Our conversations collapsed to a halt, spindled legs of sentences tapping back and forth before stuttering to stillness.

On the second day we walked from Bondi Beach to Coogee. He wore all black and went home early, close to heat stroke despite being the seasoned Aussie. Along the way, he pointed out every spider he came across, gleeful in my horror, poking at them with sticks in a childish habit he's yet to shake off. I walked several steps away from him and kept my eyes facing forward. That evening we went for burgers and mocked my parents' neurotic lunchtime search for a sandwich shop.

We travelled up the coast. A cockroach scampered over my foot at a Hawk's Nest pizzeria, and I squealed louder and higher pitched than I'm comfortable admitting. My brother then described the story of a giant huntsman in the corner of a shed in rural Queensland before his girlfriend laughed and told me how he had refused to go in there after the first time.

At the first service station, the bathroom key had a crocodile keyring the size of that fabled huntsman. I held my breath when the door swung open and welcomed that the worst thing about it was a poor tile job. On the wooded offshoots of endless roads, I stopped in restrooms that were holes in the ground yet still spider free, although in the semi dark you could hardly see the toilet. After swimming at South West Rocks, I delighted at a dolphin playing in the not-so-distant waves and walked barefoot amongst long grass. At a campsite in Byron Bay, I discovered why people get sick of kookaburras and paid very close attention to the snake warning signs. In Brisbane, I ate cheap calamari and watched a lizard climb the walls of a campervan. For the entire long drive, I squinted out the windows at the tree line in the hope of spotting a koala. By Melbourne, I'd stopped checking every corner of every room for spider nests and relaxed into a city that felt a little like home.

I came back to Sydney to see my brother again for a farewell meal, spending the last daylight hours filming the flying foxes swooping around Centennial Park. I was enchanted by how close they came, walking blindly into the trees until he called me to stop, reminding me of things that could be creeping in the undergrowth. It was worth it for the bats, for the chance to tell my brother about the swarms of them blackening the skies in Port Macquarie. Watching the fireworks over Darling Harbour, we made conversation easily, two years perhaps giving us welcome breathing space, rather than ringing the death knell of a tricky relationship.

A few days ago, my brother sent me a video of his cat chasing a spider. It's a big one for the UK, where he lives again, and a small one for Australia. Flying home from Sydney I congratulated myself on conquering a fear, but

Antarctica at Any Cost

MARIE-FRANCE ROY

Iguazú Falls, cascading into a gap between Brazil and Argentina and voted one of the New7Wonders of Nature, was merely a stopover on what was promising to be an epic, ten-week solo trip in February 2005. I was booked to go on a small cruise ship to Antarctica and had decided to visit Argentina and Uruguay on the way down.

Walking back to my guesthouse on the back streets of Puerto Iguazú, I barely noticed the young man nor the small dog trotting behind him. Soaked from the boat ride under the falls after a long day of exploring, I was looking forward to a warm shower and a good meal. Suddenly, I felt a sharp pain on my left calf.

Unnoticed, the mutt had walked over, and without any provocation, had bitten me. While I stared in utter disbelief at the bruise already forming on my leg, blood started seeping through the skin. *No, no, no, no!* I thought with a sinking feeling.

Only one week remained until my Antarctica cruise, an expensive, once-in-a-lifetime voyage I had been planning and dreaming about for an entire year, and now it seemed that the whole project could be ruined. I could contract rabies. I might need to abort my trip and go back home for treatment. With a feeling of mounting panic, I looked at the guy, pointed at my leg, and shouted in Spanish, 'Look! Look what your dog did!'

'That isn't my dog,' he replied, unconcerned. 'That dog is crazy.'

He walked away, making it clear that I would get no help from him. I was on my own.

Back at the guesthouse, I rushed into my room and washed my leg while the owner called me a taxi to go to the local clinic. By now the bite looked like a crooked smile in the middle of an angry, swelling bruise. I grabbed my vaccination card, my passport, some money, and I was off.

The little clinic was, fortunately, open on Sundays, staffed by a single nurse. She was sympathetic and cleaned my wound as best she could. Although it wasn't very deep, I was relieved I had had a tetanus shot before leaving home. What I was truly worried about, though, was rabies, but I didn't know the word in Spanish. The nurse called the doctor, and I waited for him, staring nervously at the patterns on the curtains. *This can't be happening*, I thought, feeling despondent. *Why now?*

The doctor didn't speak English either. He took a look at the bite but didn't seem too concerned. Conjuring up all the Spanish I knew, I asked him about rabies, 'You know that disease that dogs have when they foam at the mouth and go crazy?'

'Ha, *rabia!*' he said. He explained that I didn't have to worry. Rabies had been eradicated in Argentina, he said, due to systematic vaccinations.

Really? All these stray dogs have been vaccinated? How? I was dubious, but I left, limping, with gauze, tape and a prescription for painkillers and antibiotics, but no referral for rabies shots.

That night I lay in bed while all the feral dogs in the neighbourhood howled at each other. I wanted to cry. It was nearly impossible to believe that Argentina was completely rabies-free.

The following day was my birthday. 'Happy birthday to me,' I said, out loud, without much conviction. In a nearby internet café, I searched online for a good part of the morning but failed to find confirmation that rabies in Argentina had been eliminated. Finally, with mounting frustration, I emailed my travel doctor in Toronto and told him the whole story. Then I waited.

Rabies is always fatal once symptoms appear. This I knew. I was trying to stay calm and think logically. There were only three answers to this predicament: do nothing and risk dying if the local doctor was wrong; fly back home, ruin my trip, and let Canadian doctors deal with the issue; or manage it here in Argentina and hopefully keep travelling. It was obvious that this third solution made the most sense.

Walking through the town's dark and empty streets on the way to dinner became a nightmare. Dogs were *everywhere*. My heart almost stopped when a large dog inside an enclosure suddenly flung himself at the fence, barking loudly as I passed. I had never felt confident around dogs, but now I was just terrified. I drank more wine than usual with dinner to give me the courage to walk back to my guesthouse.

The following day, my heart sank when I read the Toronto doctor's reply: 'There *is* rabies in Argentina and people have died from it,' he wrote. 'Go to a clinic as soon as possible and get the rabies vaccine.' He had been nice enough to leave me the contact information of a few clinics in Buenos Aires that dealt with foreigners. I was flying in a few days, so I made an appointment with one of the clinics. My research had taught me that the vaccine needed to be administered within a week to be effective.

The doctor in Buenos Aires was very nice and spoke good English. She said that since we couldn't examine the dog, there was a chance, albeit slim, that I could have contracted rabies, so she would prescribe me the vaccine. I had never had pre-immunization, so I needed the whole series of five and each had to be administered on a specific day: days 1, 3, 7, 14 and 28.

A nurse gave me the first vaccine in the arm, as well as a gamma-globulin shot directly into the wound. Despite all the needles, I was rather relieved that everything was falling into place.

The four remaining vaccine vials were packed into a Styrofoam box along with sterilized needles, alcohol pads, and dry ice. To keep from spoiling, the vaccines had to be kept at a cool temperature for an entire month. Then I got the bill: over 1000 US dollars! Fortunately, they took credit cards. As with every trip, I had purchased medical travel insurance, which covered most of my costs in the end.

A few days later, I flew to Ushuaia, the most southerly town in the world and the starting point of my cruise. It was finally happening! The little Styrofoam box, now my most precious piece of luggage, remained top of mind. I received my second vaccine at a local clinic in Ushuaia on day 3, and after boarding the ship, I immediately asked the staff doctor to store my box in his fridge. I had made it, or so I thought.

That night, we entered the roughest sea passage in the world — the Drake Passage. The following morning, wrecked by seasickness, I found out that despite the scopolamine patch behind my ear, used to prevent motion sickness, I could not walk out of my cabin. The actual rocking motion of the ship didn't help either. My roommates had to summon the ship doctor to come over to me. He injected me in the buttock with what was apparently the strongest medication against seasickness in existence. I was feeling so ill that I didn't even care that my cabin mates were watching.

I still had to drag myself up and down the stairs between my cabin, the dining room, and the lecture hall, holding the rail with one hand and a vomit bag with the other. The ship swayed so violently at times that plates and glasses slid down tables and unsecured drawers came flying out of nightstands. Lying down was the only way to make it bearable.

The following morning, we reached Cuverville Island near the Antarctic Peninsula, and the seas finally calmed down. The ship was now gliding on perfectly flat waters, surrounded by steep cliffs, glaciers and icebergs. The landscape was stunning, even more so than what I had imagined.

Antarctica felt like a last frontier. Aside from a few research stations, it contained no man-made structures. We roamed freely on snowy and rocky islands inhabited by penguins, seals, and seabirds without seeing any sign of civilization. There were no electrical poles, no fences, and no boardwalks; our footsteps the first to break the fresh layer of snow.

We climbed a hill under fat, wet snowflakes and slid down on our bum. We hiked up the cinder cone of a collapsed volcano. We watched the penguins' antics, cute and clumsy on land but torpedo-fast underwater. On Livingston Island, petrified tree trunks and fossil ferns proved that the continent of Antarctica lay in the tropics 30 million years ago.

Motoring around the freezing waters in Zodiac boats, we came within an arm's reach of leopard seals napping on ice floes, and glistening turquoise icebergs, some the size of cathedrals. One day, a humpback whale breached right next to our inflatable craft.

After all the hardships, I now felt strong, confident, and deliriously happy to be here, at the end of the Earth. I had dealt with my fears, found a practical solution to an unpredictable issue, and made it to Antarctica.

Two weeks later in Patagonia, after my fifth and last

vaccine, I ordered a nice steak dinner accompanied by Argentinian red wine in a El Calafate restaurant. 'To the end of the rabies shots,' I said to the Universe, raising my glass and smiling. 'And to overcoming obstacles.'

The Other Side of Fear

JAIME CONLAN

The jets fly by in pairs. Every noise puts me more on edge. A door slams by accident. A motorcycle skids across the road. And even in the silence, I feel like I can still hear the sirens.

I wonder about the odds. It's the first time in five years that a missile makes it to Tel Aviv and it's the first time I'm travelling in Israel — I'm here for it. Our paths cross. I love these things; casual moments you never could have expected that become life-changing. You meet people. You see things. Things change. Missiles explode on Israel's Iron Dome.

Things change for everyone during conflict, not just for me, and I find myself repulsed by making this situation about me. I want to stop crying. I want to start acting. I cry even harder when I cycle back to the hotel and realize that it's not about me, but about the people who live every day against the odds.

I think about strong words. Retaliation, mostly ... that's a strong word. It's all I see on the Tweets from uninformed sources. Retaliation just makes me think of hurting innocent people — of fear.

Another jet flies by. I rewind. Everything replays as my brain processes something that is so novel for me yet so ordinary for everyone else. Fear tastes like normalcy to those accustomed to this world. This world of music and film and beauty, but still, missiles.

I sit here on the balcony and wait for hours, hoping to fall asleep, waiting for something to force me out of this nightmare, too tired to change anything on my own. I wonder who else has sat here wondering about war and late nights and girls singing, replaying my roommate's voice as she sang on the balcony after the missile, an attempt at self-soothing in strange lullabies.

There are some people down below on the sidewalk, and their drunkenness coats their laughter like a soft drizzle. Their laughter sings to me. It reminds me, again, of her singing. She sings to the empty balcony as the rest of us disperse into our own silos of bad coping mechanisms.

There's cigarette smoke from the balcony a few doors down. It feels like sensory overload in a vacuum — the smell of the smoke, the sound of her singing, the sweat on my palms. The missile that keeps replaying on the TV, but only for 60-seconds on CNN. Not enough to merit a longer segment.

A few days later will be different, but I don't know that then. A few days later I'll be sitting at a bar divulging my deepest fears to people I met six days ago. We'll be sitting with an Israeli filmmaker, and he'll say, 'How were the missiles?' We'll shrug and I'll awkwardly look down at my feet, embarrassed by my bout of tears from the time the sirens first went off and a stranger-turned-friend prayed over me and I debated escaping into the ocean. A missile-threat mermaid, I could be.

He'll smile at our shrugs. 'This is war. When your ex-girlfriend texts you the day after the missiles and asks, "Are you okay?" followed by, "Would you have even reached out to me to ask me if I was okay if I hadn't asked you first?"'

He'll laugh then, meet our shrugs. 'War is seeing all of your neighbours in their pyjamas. Every serious war movie ever made was made by someone who has never seen war. War is funny.'

He turns away and conversation resumes in the absence, but my mind lingers on what he says. *War is funny?*

The 'me' from a few nights ago crying on the balcony all night long could never see this possibility. The 'me' looking back on this now and the other tragedies that have followed since in Israel, Syria, Kashmir, across the world — still wrestles with this concept.

Fear, in its most amorphous, ubiquitous form, cannot dissipate so easily. I lie awake at night, wondering if it ever dies, if it ever leaves anyone alone for too long. I used to think fear and travel were opposites. Oil and water.

I was wrong beyond measure.

In the floods of all of this global fear, how do you find

humour and light? I still can't figure it out, such a far-off idea that I couldn't reach in a million years, and yet Israel teaches me. The reality. The reality is pain and fear, but it is also daily light.

It is the music. It is the beaches. It is all of the films and the books.

The beauty of it really is simple. It's waking up the next day.

Humans tend to overcomplicate things. Sometimes you don't need a solution; you just need to go to bed and try again.

The next day is beauty all over again; beauty with perhaps more depth, lined with this new realization that I'm alive, and so is everyone else, and life can be okay. Life can be the beauty of travelling to historical lands and sailing the seas.

Life is crying in a church by the Sea of Galilee, a non-religious girl finding herself in a pew with her eyes closed, crying. I cry because it's beautiful; the kind of overwhelming beauty that fills you up so much that it inevitably comes spilling out in tears. I am surrounded by a sea so cerulean blue, the brightness of it still lights up the backs of my eyelids. The flowers bloom around us. I smile, savouring the absence of fear, willing this adventure of a moment to leave me free from fear forever (in hindsight, how boring would that be?).

I look around at the faces of everyone on this trip, grateful for each one, surprised at how a group from across the USA could find ourselves in this happenstance, together.

Each person means something different to me, occupying

a very particular space in my life, each of them with their music or their craft or their charisma, creative gifts augmented by this incredible place.

Magic and laughter abound. These are the people who pray over me during crises, who talk about notating my laugh to compose its beauty, who wander around with me on small photography adventures where we run and snap pictures and smile with the fun of it all.

I find their presence helps me learn more, learn to come fearlessly into myself and the present. Our uncontrollable laughter at the dinner table starts to bind us more, and I feel myself giving in, letting loose.

So much of this trip was about giving in to a moment I could have never conceived of before, even with all of my imagination and desire to manifest wild dreams. Trying your hardest to take it all in, but everything is so overwhelmingly light and beautiful that you can't grasp it; you just have to let it pass through you and be grateful for every second of it as it comes and as it goes.

This trip was also about rediscovering an emotional rawness and connection previously lost. It was approaching the Western Wall, palms sweaty and heart beating fast, surrounded by the echoes of prayers in too many languages to count, a symphony none of us could have dreamed of composing. The moment my hand met the wall, I felt a shift and tears bubbled out of me. It was the feeling of dipping your hand into clear water on a summer day, the beginning of something, a submersion into feeling.

Of course, it wasn't all emotional impact and missiles and exploring new sights. It was humour and PikaJew T-shirts in the Old City of Jerusalem. It was waiting outside of JFC (a KFC knock-off) to make content even out of fast-food restaurants. It was the special kind of mood everyone engages with when we're all jet-lagged in a dark room at an incredible international TV conference.

The trip to Israel was all about a connection — a connection that cuts through the fear, a guiding rope out, a string that binds us all together, to each other, to the beautiful nature around us, to the works we all try to create — a song played out into the darkness.

It was the music of children in the market, the dancing of people on the streets past midnight, the smiles (god, the smiles) of everyone that I won't forget.

I had forgotten what it felt like to feel like you're finding something new, to feel like you're actually living, to have felt the fear and realize you still made it out on the other side.

Acknowledgments

I first want to thank my boss and co-editor of *Fearless Footsteps*, Nathan James Thomas. This anthology was his brainchild, and without his unwavering dedication to the final product, passion for good travel writing, and commitment to the *Intrepid Times* community, this book never would have made it to print. From the weeks of reading submissions, days of 'yes' and 'no' list-making, and hours of edits and re-edits, Nathan was there, a steady source of support and a reliable voice when it came to the tough decisions. I also want to thank members of the *Intrepid Times* community, who motivate us every day to continue publishing great travel writing. I especially want to thank the many authors of *Fearless Footsteps*, who have filled the pages of this anthology with their talent, love of travel, and enthusiasm. Their stories speak to what is human in each of us, and I'm honoured to work with such gifted writers. Finally, I want to thank our publisher, Anouska Jones, who provided consistent guidance in moments of doubt, as well as Monica Berton, who helped us through the final edits.

JENNIFER ROBERTS

This book owes a great deal to the tireless efforts of my co-editor, Jennifer Roberts, who was a major part of this project from the start, contributing her energy, diligence and editing skills to making this the book that it is. I echo the acknowledgments for the fantastically talented team at Exisle Publishing, including the wonderful Anouska Jones and, of course, Gareth St John Thomas, who decided to take a risk on this crazy little idea. We must also thank the incredibly creative authors and travellers whose words fill these pages, including those whose stories were not, in the end, selected for this anthology. Your courage to mine your own experience gives courage to others. Everyone who reads the *Intrepid Times*, follows us on social media and gives us the odd 'like' and 'share' has played their role in making this happen. I must also give a shout-out to The Coddiwomples, with whom many of my own fearless (and fearful) footsteps have been trodden, and to Joanna for your constant kindness and unwavering support throughout the challenges of taking this from idea to reality.

NATHAN JAMES THOMAS